Soul Purpose

Soul Purpose

You're Not Alone in This World

NIKKI WEBER

Dedication

To Aubry, Sydney, and Pricilla. The loves of my life! My wish for you is to experience life to its fullest, where all your dreams and wishes come true; to learn from your mistakes but not to worry about making them. Be kind and loving to all, including the trees, insects, and animals. Take risks and educate yourself as much as possible. The earth will forever teach you! Be receptive to it. Take ownership and have the power to change your circumstances. If you have questions, look within yourself for the answers, and if you feel lost, search everywhere to find yourself. For your life is to be experienced to its fullest potential. And when you look to the earth, you shall find heaven. You are children of the stars and have been created with the same captivating light. My energy will always be flowing through you. For you will always be my babies, and we will be connected eternally! Love you forever and for always!

Table of Contents

Introduction · ix

One   Refusing to Fuel Negativity · · · · · · · · · · · · · · · · · · · 1
Two   Positive and Negative Self-Talk· · · · · · · · · · · · · · · · · 5
Three   Empowerment through Taking Ownership · · · · · · · · · · 9
Four   The Power of Gratitude and Appreciation · · · · · · · · · · ·11
Five   Liberating Yourself from Approval · · · · · · · · · · · · · · ·14
Six   Mastering Our Subconscious Mind · · · · · · · · · · · · · ·19
Seven   Cultivating Self-Confidence· · · · · · · · · · · · · · · · · · ·21
Eight   Embracing the Present Moment· · · · · · · · · · · · · · · · ·23
Nine   Our Intention Creates Our Reality · · · · · · · · · · · · · · 26
Ten   Living Deliberately· ·29
Eleven   Unveiling the Truth behind Our Emotions and Our
            Guilty Feelings ·33
Twelve   Personal Development · 36
Thirteen   Working with Our Ego · 40
Fourteen   Embracing Compassion and Understanding · · · · · · · · · ·45
Fifteen   Surrendering Control· 48
Sixteen   Practicing Self-Love ·53
Seventeen   Freedom from Resentment· · · · · · · · · · · · · · · · · · · ·57
Eighteen   Welcoming Our Authentic Beauty· · · · · · · · · · · · · · · 60
Nineteen   Self-Control in Terms of Drugs, Alcohol, and
            Prescription Medications ·63
Twenty   Our Small Perspective · 68

Twenty-One   Nurturing Intimate Connections · · · · · · · · · · · · · · · · · · ·71
Twenty-Two   Finding Happiness from Within · · · · · · · · · · · · · · · · · ·76
Twenty-Three   Restoring Faith in the Goodness of Humanity· · · · · · · · ·81
Twenty-Four   Rethinking Our Values ·83
Twenty-Five   Minimizing Our Impact on the Environment · · · · · · · · ·87
Twenty-Six   Exploring Faith · 90
Twenty-Seven   Nurturing Inner Peace and Wholeness· · · · · · · · · · · · ·92
Twenty-Eight   Guiding Little Souls· 96
Twenty-Nine   Embracing Transcendence ·102
Thirty   Conclusion: The Beginning of a New Chapter· · · · · · · ·106

                Acknowledgments ·107
                Author Bio· ·111

Introduction

I wrote this book in hopes that it will influence others to have more love and compassion toward themselves and others. The ultimate goal is to encourage a shift in perspective and to help others free themselves from their negative emotions. When we cultivate positive emotions, such as gratitude, mindfulness, and self-appreciation, we have the power to transform our lives.

Additionally, this book touches upon the impact of being organized and having flexibility, self-esteem, and self-love. We also discuss the impact of social media, how we can reduce our impact on the environment and how it is OK to seek help from professionals.

I found that every chapter was relevant to my current experience, and to be honest, sometimes I felt like I was being directed by a higher force to complete this book. Our human experience is a precious one and should not be taken for granted. I hope this book serves as a guide to help you overcome the obstacles in your life, and helps you fulfill your greatest potential. You are not alone in this world, and we can all benefit positively from one another. Please read this book with an open heart and a willingness to make positive change.

One

Refusing to Fuel Negativity

Those who react without thought do not
lack sensitivity; they lack experience.

I t is very natural and a crucial part of our human existence to regularly feel negative emotions. It is how we have learned to deal with these negative emotions that dictate whether or not we can move forward from these feelings. Many of us choose to repress our negative thoughts in hopes that they will eventually disappear. However, repressing negative thoughts can be very draining on our psyche and harmful to our physical health.

There are many different situations that can leave us feeling upset, angry, jealous, frustrated, or even resentful toward others. And it is how we choose to react to these situations that will influence or affect our current state of mind. An essential part to cope with these distressing feelings is to become present and aware of the emotion. Awareness is a key component to resolving unsettling emotions, and it takes a lot of time and practice to become skilled at. In order to develop awareness, we need to guide our behavior to reflect on our thoughts and feelings.

A quote by Thema Davis states, "Those who try to break you are expecting you to be in fight mode. Conquer them with your peace." If you are not in the mindset to deal with a negative situation mindfully, be wise enough to walk away. Allowing yourself to get caught up in "fight mode" is damaging to you and the people around you. It is unlikely that there will be any amicable solution produced within an angry state of mind. If you choose to step away from the conversation, kindly let the other person know that you are not in the right state of mind to have this conversation but promise that you will come back to the issue after you have had time to think about it. *Remember*: We are not walking away from the unsettling moment with the intent of avoiding the situation; we are temporarily stepping away from the issue in order to gather our thoughts and deal with the problem more effectively.

So why is it that our happiness can be dependent on others, and why can it be so easily destroyed by someone else? I believe that it is in our true nature to want to feel a connectedness with others. When someone is unkind or mean to us, it is common for us to either become defensive or reactive. Although responding kindly is not always our first reaction, it should be the only way we choose to deal with the negativity of others. Maintaining composure will allow us to control the tone of our conversations. Shifting the tone and expressing ourselves in a nonviolent and positive way will allow us to more easily identify a solution. Harboring feelings of anger is like poisoning ourselves and expecting it to affect our enemy. It is not the other person who will suffer; it is us who will continue to suffer.

Setting boundaries and becoming assertive with those who tend to be controlling can help us maintain and establish healthier relationships. Not only with others but also with ourselves. There are many people who have never looked at themselves honestly and constantly avoid their inner issues. Instead, they tend to create drama with others, in order to avoid what is truly hurting them inside. People like this are great at avoiding their own personal issues and will likely be projecting how they feel about themselves toward you. So try not to take what others say to you too personally. Although it might seem that their anger is directed toward you, it likely has very little to do with you.

When we look at the larger scope of things and can gather our awareness, we are more likely to empathize with their position. In their time of suffering, they may never come to the realization that their problems exist within themselves and that their problems are not a result of their external environment.

Sometimes it is easier to create suffering in order to avoid traumas from the past. However, this does not mean that you can be used as a punching bag for them. That is why it is extremely important to create boundaries, which will enhance your self-esteem and help you to assert desires.

Remember that we always have the choice to either make a situation positive or make a situation negative, and negative situations are undoubtedly more draining on our systems. So, how do we go about removing these disruptive thought patterns? Well, first we need to become fully present. You can do this through mindfulness meditations. This means we need to internally reflect to resolve the problem. Start the meditation by comfortably sitting or lying down in a quiet place. Give yourself at least half an hour without distractions, and allow your mind to sit quietly. Close your eyes and focus on your breath. It is OK if thoughts become present; just gently allow them to come, evaluate them, and kindly let them pass. Now focus on the argument at hand. Maybe it is with a friend, a family member, or a coworker. Be kind to the thought and begin to ask it questions. For instance, "Why did this argument make me upset? Why does this person make me so mad? Why do I allow myself to feel upset when dealing with this person? What can I do differently in the future to change my energy toward this person? Does this person have any positive qualities?" Make sure to answer each question honestly and with a loving heart. Then slowly shift your questioning to a more sympathetic tone. By changing your tone, your perspective regarding the situation should shift, allowing you to confront the problem in a more empathetic way. For example, is it possible that "so and so" is having trouble in their own lives? Maybe they have lost a loved one recently? Maybe they are struggling financially? Maybe they had a bad childhood, or maybe they were bullied their whole lives? The answers to these questions are not excusing the individual's bad behavior; it is only allowing us to look at the individual in a different light. Practicing mindful meditations when dealing with problematic people will eventually change your energy toward them, allowing you to confront this person in a different manner.

When we are upset with someone, we should try to remind ourselves that, like us, they are only trying to attain happiness. Our words and the way we conduct ourselves have the ability to either bring people up or bring people down. Let's choose to build each other up. It is an effortless choice to love one another, to rejoice in another's happiness, and to be grateful for those who are kind to us. Hate will only cause tears, heartache, and suffering, and once we become more aware of the things that make us happy, we will more easily be able to identify the things that do not make us happy. Avoid those individuals who choose to belittle others, are self-entitled, and utilize criticism to boost their own energy. People who are fixated on negative events do not have our best interest at heart; therefore, it is in our best interest to instead surround ourselves with like-minded optimists.

When we choose to switch our attention to the kind things that people do rather than the inhumane acts of those who are starving for attention, our inner dialogue will shift to a more positive one. Who knows, maybe those who thrive on creating drama will try to manage themselves differently because we have. Energy is contagious, and our reactions can easily influence the reactions of others. So if someone yells at you, instead of yelling back, try saying "Hey, I understand you're upset and I'm willing to listen to you, but would you be open to discuss this in an hour when we're both less angry?" I guarantee, you are going to have a far deeper and more connected conversation than if you chose to yell back. Because when we yell, we are not listening or receiving information; we are only trying to be heard.

Two

Positive and Negative Self-Talk

What is held in mind tends to manifest.

—David R. Hawkins

Although it is true that others can cause stress in our lives, the main cause of our unhappiness lies within our inner dialogue. Positive and negative self-talk has a real impact on the way we feel about ourselves and our external experiences. It has been proven time and time again that if we choose to look at a situation differently, we can then alter our perception. For instance, the anxiety and stress you feel prior to taking an exam keeps you from sleeping and thinking clearly and, even worse, can affect your biochemistry negatively. Now try to replace that negative thought with a positive one such as excitement. With practice, our experience will eventually shift to being positive.

We also seem to constantly be stressing about our first world problems. More than ever, we seem to have an obsession with our bodies and the vanities of life. We worry about gaining a few pounds, getting zits, and how many likes we will receive on social media. Our bodies do not define who we are and should not validate how we feel about ourselves. Our bodies are only the physical part of ourselves, and yes, we should take care of it by eating healthy, not overindulging, and drinking lots of water, but we should also do the same for our souls. In essence, we are our bodies, but we are also souls. Taking care of both is essential to feeling good about ourselves. Of course, it feels nice when someone likes a photo that we posted, but it also makes us feel badly when we do not receive any feedback. Unfortunately, our younger generations are experiencing a lot of stress and negative self-perceptions due to their online experiences. Now it is more important than ever to cultivate a positive self-image, and we can do this by meditating regularly, utilizing our creative outlets, enjoying social time with friends, exercising regularly, and practicing positive affirmations. This way we will have a solid internal foundation when we choose to share pieces of our lives with the outside world. Not requiring validation for our posts but instead feeling happy, we shared something positive with our friends and family, regardless of how many "likes" we might receive. There is no doubt that the lives of today's generation revolve around social media. These platforms definitely have their fair share of benefits if utilized properly and not obsessively. We can stay in touch with loved ones across the country, have conference calls no matter where we are, keep up-to-date on traffic delays and listen to our favorite musicians anytime anywhere, but these outlets can also become very addictive and segregate us from the real world. Rather than always texting, try picking up the phone or actually physically meeting someone to chat. Make time during the day to meditate and allocate a portion of your day to doing something outside. Say hi to your neighbor or spark up a conversation with someone in the elevator. Do not be afraid of the outside world; we are all striving for similar goals, and sometimes the most purposeful conversations are the ones we have on the fly. Life can be exciting, as long as we choose to live in the *now* and not allow our fears or negative self-talk to dictate how our lives should be lived. You have no idea how many times I have caught someone off guard with a friendly hello and in turn learned something new and interesting.

Although social media can be responsible for many of our deluded thought patterns, we cannot play the blame game. Again, it is our choice what we choose to tune in to and how we choose to interpret that information. Negative self-talk such as "I need to be perfect," "I need at least one hundred likes," and "I can never take a good picture" are thoughts that we have pre-programmed into our own brains. These thoughts are completely normal, and each one of us has experienced low self-esteem at some point in our lives, but it does not mean that we should keep telling ourselves these lies. As long as we can be present and be aware when these thoughts appear, we can then change the behavior. Negative self-talk and the stresses related to it can be overwhelming on our mental health. Limiting our negativity and challenging the damaging thought can dissolve its influence.

However, not all stress is negative stress. Planning a wedding, having a baby, buying a new house, or planning a family vacation can be considered positive stress. Keeping a clear and open mind to change will be very beneficial in these times of excitement. As we all know, things do not always go the way we imagined, but sometimes things change for the better. Releasing our attachments to a specific outcome can allow things to flow naturally, and in my personal experience, this is always the best way to plan. The universe always knows exactly what you need. Nonetheless, negative stresses such as divorce or losing a job still occur all the time. These stresses can lead to serious health implications, exhaustion, and consume our minds with negative self-talk. We need to be mindful when caring for these stressful emotions in order to deal with them properly. Since everyone's therapeutic needs are different, there are various methods of cognitive restructuring (CR) that have been proven to alter our negative self-talk.

The cognitive restructuring is a psychotherapeutic process of learning to identify and dispute irrational or maladaptive thoughts known as cognitive distortions. These cognitive distortions can easily be redirected with practice. When a dysfunctional thought pattern becomes present, there are many mood repair strategies that you can utilize to help you cope with the negative thought pattern. Exercise has been proven to release tension and has the ability to increase your self-confidence. With regular practice, your whole mood will shift. You will regain new energy in your life, you will be able to direct your negative feelings constructively, and you will definitely feel better about yourself. Another method would be to retrain your brain. We all have pre-conditioned thought patterns that regularly occur, yet they hold no validity.

Those thoughts have literally been programmed into our internal dialogue. With time and practice, we can choose to shift that preconditioned thought to a more uplifting one. For example, when the thought of "I'm ugly" comes to mind, you need to shift that thought to "I'm beautiful." For every single thought of "I'm ugly," replace it with ten thoughts of "*I am beautiful.*" Then focus on what you like about yourself—your eyes, your personality, your intellect, your kind heart, your nice butt. There are a million things you can love about yourself. Choose to focus on the positive things about yourself.

I have learned that every negative reaction has an equal positive reaction. It is our choice which perspective we choose. Remember, we are in control of our own lives and must liberate ourselves from our fears. Looking at the worst-case scenario and analyzing it mindfully can eliminate our doubts and help us focus on the realities of the situation. Sometimes our worst-case thoughts can limit us from doing the things we might enjoy, but when we look at the reality of these thoughts, we come to the realization that these thoughts are very unlikely to occur. It is just like the child that refuses to eat something new, but when they try it, they discover something new that they love.

The next step to healing is trusting ourselves. Trust your intuitions and do not allow others to steal your power or make you think you are the crazy one. You know yourself the best, so do what is best for you. If you are unhappy in a relationship, leave. If you feel as if you are not being treated fairly at work, make changes. Life on earth does not last forever, so make every second worth it. We all deserve to be happy, and we all have the power to make happiness happen in our own lives. Have the courage to make changes and embrace the excitement of something different and challenging.

Three

Empowerment through Taking Ownership

One can only truly be happy once one is true with one's self.

Sometimes it is easier to blame others for our unhappiness than it is to take ownership for our own circumstances. We need to consider that our lives are the way they are because we have chosen for it to be this way. Everything that we experience in the world is a reflection of ourselves. If we are angry, we will encounter angry environments, but if we are happy, we will encounter happy environments.

Taking ownership and realizing that we have caused the mass majority of our own problems is exhilarating. This epiphany allows us to take back control in our own lives. The most gratifying feeling in the world is feeling happy, and we can only do this when we fully understand that we control the way we feel and react. If we choose to react negatively, we will feel negative, but if we choose to react positively, we will feel positive.

Questioning our reasoning for blaming others is an excellent mediation exercise. For instance, if we have anger toward our sister, it might be helpful to think of things such as "Why can't I be happy for my sister? Why do I feel jealousy toward her? How can I change my perception in order to change those negative feelings?" Think deeply on where this resentment might stem from. Mediate on each one of these thoughts and allow all thoughts to flow freely and do not try to force a solution. The solution will come naturally as long as we are taking ownership for the change and betterment of ourselves.

It seems to be easier to blame others for our problems than it is to take responsibility, but this is not true. By blaming others, we are giving them the power to control us. When we have discouraging thoughts such as "Because of so and so, my life is miserable," we allow external forces to influence our attitudes. Instead, we need to change our statement to "Since so and so is not a positive force in my life, how can I limit my connection to them?" or "What type of changes can I make in my life that can free me from caring what so and so thinks of me?" or "What can I do differently when dealing with so and so, so that I can regain control over my own life?"

I find that we often choose to repress these thoughts because they make us feel uncomfortable. Understanding that everyone has experienced some form of jealousy or hatred might help us feel more comfortable analyzing these distressing thoughts. There is a connectedness in knowing that others have experienced these same problems. When we repress an emotion, it does not go away. If we face that emotion and question it, this is when we can resolve the problem. All problems start from within, and all problems can be resolved from within. However, sometimes our issues are so deeply rooted that it may be best to consult a professional to help us conquer them. Never be afraid to contact a therapist or counselor if your issues seem too big to tackle on your own. It can be equally as beneficial to have a third party's perspective.

Once we choose to take ownership for our own happiness, we realize we are in total control of our own emotions. Of course, we will still feel negative emotions on occasion, but these emotions are only temporary, as is everything in the universe. Be kind to yourself and understand that you are in charge of yourself and the way you choose to feel. When you feel sad, try to evoke feelings of happiness; when you feel angry, try to evoke feelings of kindness. Take back control of your own life. No one should dictate how your day will go but you.

Four

THE POWER OF GRATITUDE AND APPRECIATION

Gratitude can transform common days into thanksgivings, turn routine jobs into joy and change opportunities into blessings

— WILLIAM ARTHUR WARD

In challenging times, it is very difficult to be grateful; however, this is the most important time to practice our gratitude. When our beautiful daughter was born, she had serious acid reflux, making her very uncomfortable, which in turn made her scream in pain for up to six hours a day. Doctors told us that it was "colic" and that it could last anywhere from four to eight months. It was so hard to watch her scream in agony for hours, and it was absolutely draining for my son, my husband, and me. Especially knowing that there was nothing we could do to take away her pain. The first couple of months are a complete blur for me. Constantly trying anything and everything to keep her comfortable was exhausting for us all. On top of the constant screaming, our sweet little girl developed a serious cold. As did I and my son. The whole situation was unbearable, and the only things that got us through it were (1) realizing that the situation was temporary, (2) being grateful for the support we were able to give one another, (3) thanking God that we were not dealing with a more serious health concern, (4) being thankful she was sleeping through the nights, (5) and, finally, praying to God and being grateful for the positive things in our life. Of course, there were many moments where we took our frustrations out on each other, but being grateful for our strong relationship helped us overcome our challenges. When we started looking at our situation with gratitude, we began to see things differently. Our beautiful baby girl was born healthy and had a family that loved her more than anything. There is no doubt that our situation was minuscule in comparison to a family dealing with a child born with a more serious health concern. Nonetheless, it was still a challenge that we had to face together.

In times of suffering, it is pertinent to recognize all the things we are grateful for. Even being grateful for the little things is a beautiful way to start. Thank the universe, God, or whomever you worship for the delicious breakfast in front of you. Be thankful for waking up in a warm bed or getting three healthy meals a day. Sadly, we can live in a world where we regularly take advantage of these small luxuries. But did you know that there are over 350 children who die every hour from hunger. Think about how grateful they would be to have even one of those meals a day. Most of us live very fortunate lives and should not take anything for granted. If we are lucky enough to have a roof over our heads, a job that provides income, and clean drinking water, we have literally won the lottery of life.

Try starting or ending your day off with a small prayer of gratitude. This is an example of mine.

Dear God, guardian angels, and spirits around me, I am so thankful that I am healthy and happy. I am so grateful that my family is happy and healthy. Thank you for the great life you have provided for me. Thank you for always leading me in the right direction, and thank you for always protecting me from evil. Please shine a bright light on my son, my daughters, my husband, and our animals. Please protect them from evil and help guide them in the right direction. Please help those in need, and please end any suffering they may be struggling with so they too can feel a sense of peacefulness. Thank you, God, for everything; I feel so blessed and lucky to be living this life. God bless us all.

I use God because it is a term I feel comfortable with. But you do not have to believe in a God to be grateful. Maybe you are an atheist, or maybe you are very spiritual. It really does not matter. Gratitude does not care what your religious belief is. I tell my kids to write down five things they are grateful for each day, and I myself practice a guided gratitude meditation each day for ten minutes. It takes very little effort but has major benefits.

Appreciation is a major component of gratitude. Showing appreciation to others can not only make you feel good about yourself but also make the receiver feel good about themselves. It is scientifically proven that practicing gratitude can boost your immune system. In an article published on positive-phycology.com, it states that when we express gratitude and receive the same, our brain releases dopamine and serotonin, the two crucial neurotransmitters responsible for our emotions. They enhance our mood immediately, making us feel happy from the inside. It proves that grateful people are typically less angry in their own lives and are able to cultivate more feelings of love and kindness.

Overall, we know from experience how good it makes us feel when our kindness is recognized, so in turn we should not take anything for granted. Let us choose to be grateful when the sun shines because it provides nourishment to the earth. Let us choose to be grateful when it rains because our plants will thrive. Let us choose to be grateful when it snows because it makes everything look so beautiful and hides those cute little white rabbits from predators. Let us do our best to recognize the good in all situations and appreciate those who help us live our best lives.

Five

Liberating Yourself from Approval

While feeling appreciated is a healthy thing, feeling a need to seek out approval from people in our lives is quite the opposite.

—Hale Dwoskin

Often we choose to conform to what others want us to be. Meaning that we are constantly putting off our own tasks and setting aside our personal beliefs in order to please those around us. Do you regularly find yourself canceling things that are important to you to help those around you? Have you ever compromised your morals just to feed in to someone else's ego? If so, it is possible that you might be addicted to the approval of others. This is nothing to be ashamed of. I myself used to live of a life addicted to the approval of others. I often found myself bailing on my closest friends or family members just to receive the approval of a stranger. I absolutely hated it when someone did not like me and would do everything in my power to shift their opinions of me. I was constantly saying yes to other's demands even though I was completely oblivious of my own schedule. I was literally living my life to please others, and in turn, I was starving myself of any dignity or self-worth. After the burnout of an unorganized and chaotic schedule, I came to the realization that self-care and self-love should be my priority. It is OK to want to help others, but we need to help ourselves first.

For instance, let us say you have a friend (Shiela) who is recently single and has two kids. "Shiela" has started asking you (last minute) to take her kids for the weekend while she enjoys her new single life. Being sympathetic to her needs, you say yes. However, now you seem to be taking care of "Shiela's" kids more often than she does, and you feel as though you are being taken advantage of. Regardless of your feelings, you continue to say yes time and time again, until it gets to a point where you start icing her phone calls and avoiding the situation. If this sounds familiar, you are not alone. I have experienced this time and time again. Deep down, we might feel like our kindness is being taken advantage of, but we do not have the courage to say no. But when we truly look at this situation, is saying no such a bad thing? *No*, it is not! There are a million kinds of ways that we can say no without offending "Shiela."

"Hey, Shiela, I'm so flattered that you would ask me to take your kids again, but we have dinner plans. I'm so sorry I can't help."

"Hey, Shiela, would it be OK if I got back to you after I check my schedule? I feel like I might have something planned for those days."

"Unfortunately we're not available those days."

"Wish we could, but we have plans."

It is not rude to have a life of your own. Sure, "Shiela" is your friend, and you would like to help her out, but you should not feel an obligation to her responsibilities. People-pleasing can be very damaging to our souls. Although it is a good thing to live our lives in a way that benefits others, it is not a good thing to constantly be sacrificing our own schedules to please the "Shielas" of the world. There needs to be a healthy balance of tending to other's needs and taking care of ourselves.

Our decisions should be based on what is best for our higher selves. Yes, sometimes that means choosing things that will disappoint others, but we have to be OK with that. We cannot please 100 percent of the people 100 percent of the time. That is a completely asinine statement and absolutely impossible! Being our authentic selves and having the confidence to be who we are is what makes us special.

If we were all the same, life would be dull and boring. Being different is what draws us to one another. One of the most attractive qualities a person can have is when they are confident enough to be vulnerable. Often we will associate vulnerability with weakness, but it is quite the opposite. Surrendering our fears of not being accepted and allowing our true feelings to come forward is very empowering. It is incredibly uplifting when we can express our true feelings without being concerned about what others think of us.

We are only cheating ourselves and others by being resistant to vulnerability. If we are unhappy in a relationship but have chosen to stay because we do not want to let that person down, or maybe we are afraid of how they might respond, neither party will benefit from the relationship. Have you ever thought that maybe you are unhappy in your relationship because you are afraid to express yourself honestly and that maybe they are also hurting because subconsciously they know the truth? Believe it or not, we are all very connected and have the ability to pick up on each other's energies. Even if that emotion is unspoken. It is best for everyone involved to be open and honest with one another, and we should not be afraid to open up about our feelings.

Moscow's hierarchy is a great way to regain your self-confidence and a good way to help us live a more self-actualizing life. Becoming self-actualizing is not easily attained, and I would be totally surprised if it has ever been perfected. I personally interpret it as maintaining a level of trueness to one's self.

An article posted on <u>healthline.com</u> that was medically reviewed by <u>Timothy J. Legg, Ph.D., CRNP</u>—written by <u>Crystal Raypole</u> on February 26, 2020, called "A (Realistic) Guide to Becoming Self-Actualized"—referred to steps that we can take in order to help us live a more self-actualizing life based on Maslow's hierarchy. The article stated:

(Start Quote) Generally speaking, self-actualized people:

- Live independently. They don't structure their lives around the opinions of others. They may not seem swayed by social feedback. They also have an appreciation for solitude and don't always need company.
- Have a sense for reality and truth. They may seem more grounded and in touch with actual possibilities and have an easier time detecting falseness from other people.
- Are comfortable with the unknown. They don't mind not knowing what the future holds.
- Have compassion, kindness, and acceptance. This goes both for themselves and for others they encounter.
- Have a good-natured sense of humor. They can laugh at themselves when they make mistakes and help others see humor in challenging situations.
- Enjoy meaningful friendships. They tend to build long-lasting relationships with a few people instead of casual friendships with many people.
- Have a sense of spontaneity. They live more naturally, rather than in a rigid way, and aren't afraid to follow what happens in the moment instead of sticking to routine.
- Are creative. Creativity doesn't just refer to artistic abilities. Some self-actualized people might have a knack for looking at problems in new ways or thinking along different lines than other people do. They may simply lack inhibition, another characteristic of a spontaneous nature.
- Enjoy peak experiences. A peak experience describes a moment of euphoria, wonder, and joy, often characterized by a sense of feeling connected to the universe. They might seem like eye-opening moments, where deeper meanings suddenly become clear. They aren't necessarily spiritual, though.

- Focus on things bigger than themselves. They tend to see the big picture instead of only considering their own lives, and may dedicate their lives to a mission, cause, or deeper purpose.
- Stop and smell the roses. They appreciate each positive or joyful moment — a sunrise, a partner's kiss, a child's laugh — as if it were the first, no matter how many times they've already experienced it.
- Have a sense of justice. They have compassion and care for all people, and work to prevent acts of injustice or unethical behavior.
- Possess Gemeinschaftsgefühl, or "social feeling." This word, coined by Alfred Adler, describes an interest and concern for the general well-being of other humans.

If all of this feels unattainable, remember that self-actualization is a process, not an endgame. There's no single point where you "should" end up on the journey. (End Quote)

This technique is one of many that can help us set boundaries and regain our self-confidence. It does not mean that we have to perfect all of the above, but it is likely that we already possess a few of these qualities. Having a solid foundation and a general guideline to work toward helps us achieve the goal of feeling peace in not needing to please others.

Six

MASTERING OUR SUBCONSCIOUS MIND

*When we become fixated on our perceptions,
we lose our ability to fly.*

Our subconscious mind is at the forefront of the majority of our problems. If we have not yet developed the ability to tap into self-awareness, it can create serious problems in our lives. Those who are subconsciously self-sabotaging are always making excuses for themselves and are completely ambivalent of their actions and how they are contributing to their own unhappiness.

When we ignore our negative emotions, we are more likely to play the blame game and are definitely more likely to criticize others. When others try to help, the self-sabotaged mind will always make an excuse: "It's too far," "I don't have time," "My life is too busy," "They're going to steal my idea," "I can't trust anyone," and so forth. This is because deep down (subconsciously) the self-sabotaged mind does not feel that it deserves stress relief or any level of happiness. Generally speaking, there is likely a deep underlying issue pertaining to self-worth that needs to be examined. If we are willing to put in the time and effort, we will eventually gain the courage to face these negative emotions. There are many guided meditations on the internet or in yoga practices that can help us release subconscious blockages. These meditations can be highly beneficial in changing our attitude and allow us to confront unsettling emotions in a peaceful state of mind.

For it is our collective thought that creates bad events. If we choose to only see the good, there will only be good. Do not give energy elsewhere, for it is like creating cancer in your own body. Our thoughts have the ability to manifest into reality. Feed only the positive ones and give no energy to the negative ones. In every situation, there is good to be found. Although sometimes it seems difficult to find, if we search deep enough, love will always appear!

A quote by author 50 Cent in his book *The 50th Law* gives us a new perspective regarding our emotions and the events that create them: "Events in life are not negative or positive. They are completely neutral. The universe does not care about your fate. It is indifferent to the violence that may hit you or to death itself. Things merely happened to you. It is your mind that chooses to interpret them as negative or positive."

We need to live in moments of self-discovery. When something seems wrong, take it as an opportunity to discover something new. Similar to in-flight safety protocol where the flight attendant advises us to first secure our oxygen masks before assisting a child or someone else, it is essential that we first care for ourselves before we can be valuable to someone else.

Seven

CULTIVATING SELF-CONFIDENCE

*That voice you call intuition is your
soul talking. You can trust it.*

—NIKKI WEBER

There is an invisible energy that affects the world around us. We all vibrate at different frequencies, and these frequencies can be emitted outward, but we can also emit them inward. When we internalize negative energy, the buildup can have serious implications on our health and our minds. If we search deeply within ourselves to resolve this buildup of energy, it will dissolve into nothingness. Once this negative energy has dissolved, we can then allow space for more positive healing thoughts.

When we believe in the power of our minds and the effects that it has on our well-being and our bodies, we can then accept the fact that we have the power to choose—whether we want to feel healthy or whether we want to feel sick. Do not confuse this treatment with rejecting modern medicine. Modern medicine is extremely beneficial in treating all sorts of illnesses and should always be used in conjunction with a positive mindset. The belief that we can mentally shift our biology is a powerful tool that should be utilized to assist in our healing processes.

So when we realize that our environments affect our genetic activity, we will naturally start to choose interactions that are uplifting to our souls. Rather than listening to that old friend complain over and over again about how shitty their life is, maybe you choose to ignore their call and instead go to a spin class or discover a new trail with a more positive friend. You know those people who lift you up rather than bring you down? They are the ones we want to surround ourselves with.

If your emotions are hung up on an old fling, try deleting them from your contact list, burn old love letters, or for a more physical release, try enrolling in a boxing class or booking yourself into a Reiki session. Another great way to mentally release any attachment is to envision a rope connecting you to the other person and then imagining yourself cutting that rope and allowing yourself and the other person to be free. Once these emotional attachments are released, we can allow ourselves to become more present and start to focus on activities and people who make us feel expansive.

The ultimate cure for our pain, whether it be emotional or physical, is when we finally start to love ourselves and our bodies. Tuning into our bodies and listening to the information it is so clearly communicating will allow us to take better care of ourselves. If we have been working hard all day and our knees start to ache, realize that this pain is a clear sign that we need to take a break. Drink some water, or even consider revisiting the project another day. Our pain is telling us what our body needs. *Listen* to it! When we can more clearly identify what our limits are, our bodies will respond positively.

However, we should not feel discouraged if we eventually find ourselves falling back into old habits or thought patterns. It takes patience and trust in ourselves to experience a shift in our self-perceptions, and once we experience the results, there is no turning back. As my husband always says, "It takes twenty-one days or longer to change a habit." So when we have identified with a certain way of being for so long, it will take time for us to learn it differently, but as long as we have faith and determination, our conditions will eventually heal themselves.

Eight

EMBRACING THE PRESENT MOMENT

We are all waking up! It is an unavoidable epidemic.

If we pay attention to the state of things as they are, we can experience each moment as it comes. Pay close attention to the leaves on the trees. See if you can separate one from the other, watch them dance in the wind, and notice that each tree holds its own energy, which it shares with the world. Not only is it magnificent, but it is humble enough to donate its oxygen to us. Without it, we would not be alive. Notice how its leaves flip when it senses rain or how quickly its leaves turn color come fall. Acknowledging and being grateful for the small details within our surroundings can help us identify with the present moment. Rather than seeking out fabricated information in the cyber world, try focusing on the environment around you. What can you feel? What can you smell? What can you taste? Experiencing real-life moments as they come is how we become present. It is that easy.

Constantly living in our own heads and creating fearful events does not get us very far. Does it? I once heard a wise man say, "Life is not about waiting for the storm to end; it is about wanting to dance in the rain." If we go with the flow, there are endless possibilities. Spontaneity will bring endless opportunities our way.

I can personally recall being five months pregnant with my third, with hormones raging, struggling within my marriage, dwelling on negative thoughts, and finally saying to myself, "*Stop!* It's time to take a break." Trust me; it was not the ideal time. Actually, it could not have been the worst timing. We had family coming to stay with us from out of province, my husband was working, and I had a one-year-old and a twelve-year-old to take care of. Nonetheless, my mind was negatively racing out of control, and I was not living in the present moment. Despite everything that was happening that day, I decided it was best to take a "*me*" day. I took my twelve-year-old (Angel) to his dad's and asked my husband to pick up our precious one-year-old from day care. I cleaned the house for our guests, washed their beds, picked up an easy dinner for my husband to prepare, then headed off to a spa in the mountains. I was seriously hesitant, but after forcing my CC numbers to confirm my booking, I obviously had no choice but to commit, and I am so grateful that I did. When I finally arrived, I felt this instant release of all my stresses. The room was stunning, and the people were so friendly. It was the break I needed and absolutely deserved.

Even though I had not ridden a bike in ages, I decided to rent one and tour the scene. The mountain views were gorgeous, and the energy was incredibly calming. I found a bench overlooking a golf course in the middle of the mountains, and while I sat there surrounded by nature, I finally started to feel at peace. My mind was able to stop racing, and my negative perspectives started to disappear. During this calmness, I could look at my thoughts without my negative thought patterns diluting my perspectives. I could be present in that moment and reflect on all the positive moments in my life. It was then that I realized that in this peaceful state of mind, it was much easier to come up with constructive solutions to my problems.

It is normal to lose touch with reality when we get caught up in our busy schedules. Rushing from one task to another and pushing thoughts or important conversations to the side can have us feeling flustered without knowing why. When we avoid our reality, it is easy to become transfixed within our negative thought patterns. But when we become present, we can fully identify with our true emotions without our negative perceptions interfering with the solution. When we have the ability to calm our minds and become present, we can begin to look at our situations in a different mindset—which, in turn, helps us gather the strength to deal with these problems in a more constructive manner.

Nine

Our Intention Creates Our Reality

Focus on heaven rather than on earth.

—The Bible

When we have absorbed a negative attitude toward the world, it becomes challenging to feel happy. The news, social media, social crises (e.g., coronavirus pandemic), and the people we surround ourselves with have a huge impact on the way we choose to look at our day. For example, the media can have a huge negative impact on our worldview perceptions. They have the ability to control and manipulate the way we see things, and unfortunately, they choose to focus mainly on the negative events occurring in the world. This is something I like to call "trash in, trash out."

If all we do is focus on the negative, then all we have to contribute is negative. This does not mean we have to completely omit social media or news from our lives, but I am suggesting that you choose to limit your exposure to it. A good way to wean yourself off these negative channels is by choosing a time of day when you can catch up. For example, during lunch hour, give yourself half an hour to quickly check your Facebook and news outlets, but that is it. I would also suggest not doing this first thing in the morning or before you go to bed, since these messages can set the tone for your day.

I have personally deleted any social media outlets that I have found to be negatively impacting my time or my mind and have made a choice not to watch the news. Instead, I choose to tune in to a more positive outlet, such as morning meditations, my favorite shows, my kids, daily affirmations, my animals, and writing.

Instead of tuning in to these negative outlets during your free time, try texting your partner a sweet note or send a fun photo of the kids to your parents. Trust me, quitting social media and turning the news off will not infringe on your social life. Actually, it will do quite the opposite. You will find that you will start to connect with your family and friends on a deeper level and actually have the physical time to spend with them.

Try affirmations such as "I am worth it," "I love myself," "I am so lucky to have what I have," "I deserve to be happy because I am not my past, nor should I be concerned with the future," "I choose to be happy today, and I choose to extend all my love to the world," "I choose to accept any love that will come my way and choose to look at each moment as though it may be my last," "I will look at every moment as positively as possible, and I will love myself!"

Keep in mind that just because we say an affirmation, it does not mean it will automatically come true. Committing to a daily affirmation is an invitation to help us believe these statements wholeheartedly. After saying them so, often your body and brain begin believing in their truths, and that is when the true magic happens.

Here are some affirmations to get you started:

- I am healthy.
- I am happy.
- I am loved.
- I deserve love.
- I am relaxed.
- I am confident.
- I am decisive.

- I know what I want.
- I know exactly what my true purpose is.
- I communicate my feelings with others softly and directly.
- Everything I need comes easily and effortlessly.
- Today is a great day.

Ten

Living Deliberately

You will not discover your life purpose by looking within yourself. You can discover your true nature that way, but purpose is only fulfilled beyond our self-centredness.

It is incredibly easy to go through life neglecting to realize that life might have a greater meaning than the monotony of each day. We often do not stop to think about what the sole purpose of living might be. Have you ever stopped to think about why you decided to take on a certain profession, have children, or strive to obtain a certain social status? Thinking about our values, beliefs, and behaviors will help us transcend into a different way of being. When we start to transform our daily experiences and truly observe our actions, sometimes we realize we are only existing and not truly living.

When we stop conforming to the norm and move away from our robotic thought patterns, we open the door of expansion and can feed our curiosity, freeing the mind and soul from internal clutter and allowing space for the things that will uplift us. It is very normal to feel hopeless when it comes to moving beyond certainty, but hopelessness is what will lead to the discovery of our purpose. Becoming uncomfortable can really inspire new energy and reconstruct what we choose to make important in our lives.

To find meaning and purpose in our lives, we need to feel connected to the present moment, ourselves, and to others. In order to feel present, we need to lift ourselves out of our daily chaos and create a balanced schedule. Scheduling will help us slow down and feel more organized, helping us to become more present in the *now*. First, try to create a schedule based on your current *"to-do list."*—for instance, work, kids, dinner, and anything else you can think of that would be considered a normal daily activity. Next, create a list of the things you would like to add to your daily rituals—for example, mediation, acupuncture, exercise, painting class, spending quality time with friends or family. When contemplating what you would like to make time for, try to discover the things that you would like to improve on. Would you like to meditate more? Would you like to follow through and complete a project? Would you like to be nicer? Would you like to be stronger? Would you like to stress less or talk less? Once you have pinned down what you would like to improve on and your schedule has become an effortless one, you can then start adding the things you would like to make time for. Slowly add one activity at a time until it feels natural. I have added a mock schedule below to give you an example.

JANUARY 2022

Sunday	Monday	Tuesday	Wednesday	Thursday	Friday	Saturday
26	27	28	29	30	31	Meditate 5 am 1 Son's basketball 3:15 Dinner with Dad
2 Meditate 5:00 am	Meditate 5 am 3 Daycare 8 am Gym 8:30 - 10 Garbage	Meditate 5 am 4 cleaner @ 12:00 free day with kids	Meditate 5 am 5 Daycare 8 am Gym 8:30 - 10 Basketball 6 - 7	Meditate 5 am 6 Daycare 8 am Basketball 6 - 7	Meditate 5 am 7 Gym 8:30 - 10 grocery friends house	Meditate 5 am 8 Yard chores
9 Meditate 5:00 am	Meditate 5 am 10 Daycare 8 am Gym 8:30 - 10 Blue Bin	Meditate 5 am 11 free day with kids	Meditate 5 am 12 Daycare 8 am Gym 8:30 - 10 Basketball 6 - 7	Meditate 5 am 13 Daycare 8 am Yoga 9 - 10 Basketball 6 - 7	Meditate 5 am 14 Gym 8:30 - 10 zoo Groomer	Meditate 5 am 15 Gardening Nails 11 am
16 Meditate 5:00 am Dinner @ Frans	Meditate 5 am 17 Daycare 8 am Gym 8:30 - 10 Garbage	Meditate 5 am 18 cleaner @ 12:00 free day with kids	Meditate 5 am 19 Daycare 8 am Gym 8:30 - 10 Basketball 6 - 7	Meditate 5 am 20 Daycare 8 am Yoga 9 - 10 Basketball 6 - 7	Meditate 5 am 21 Camping	22 Camping
23 Camping	Meditate 5 am 24 Daycare 8 am Gym 8:30 - 10 Blue Bin	Meditate 5 am 25 free day with kids	Meditate 5 am 26 Daycare 8 am Gym 8:30 - 10 Basketball 6 - 7	Meditate 5 am 27 Daycare 8 am Yoga 9 - 10 Basketball 6 - 7	Meditate 5 am 28 Gym 8:30 - 10 grocery friends over	Meditate 5 am 29
30 Meditate 5:00 am	Meditate 5 am 31 Daycare 8 am Gym 8:30 - 10 Garbage	1	2	3	4	5

As the example illustrates, meditation is something I wanted to create more time for, wistfully having to sacrifice my "shut-eye" but eventually becoming accustomed to the early mornings. Once you have your daily schedule sorted, you will have a clearer vision where you can add your "want to"s. Also, keep in mind that once a week, you should allocate a day when you can schedule quality time with your kids (whether they are grown or not). If you do not have kids, make time for family or friends. Another essential rule to note is to be flexible when it comes to your schedule. If things change, do not stress about it. Just allow it to come in and flow with the process. I find when you open up to flexibility, the universe will always work in your favor.

Now that we have organized our minds and can clearly see where we have space, we can allow God/the universe/whatever your higher power might be in order to utilize our energies to serve the greater good. This is essentially what our purpose will be. We all have different routes that make it virtually impossible to measure how successful we have become when achieving our life's purpose. This is an individual journey that we must strive to achieve on our own. So why were you put on this earth, and are you fulfilling your purpose? I struggled with this question my entire life, but it was because I was comparing myself to others and had unrealistic goals for myself that left me lost. That is, until I came across this.

Good Karma

"What is my purpose in life?" I asked the void.

"What if I told you that you fulfilled it when you took an extra hour to talk to that kid about his life?"

"Or, when you paid for that young couple in the restaurant? Or, when you saved that dog in traffic? Or, when you tied your father's shoes for him?"

"Your problem is that you equate your purpose with goal-based achievement. The universe isn't interested in your achievements . . . just your heart. When you choose to act out of kindness, compassion, and love, you are already aligned with your true purpose."

"No need to look any further!"

After reading that statement, I realized that I have been fulfilling my purpose all along. No, I was not volunteering, creating something to improve the quality of the earth, or running a multimillion-dollar business. I am a mother fulfilling the needs of my children; picking up garbage when I see it in my community; talking to literally everyone I see, because you never know what kind of day they are having; always smiling and very optimistic; rescuing animals without hesitation; being kind to all living beings, including the plants; recycling as much as possible; being a good friend and neighbor; not being judgmental to those around me; and, most of all, trying to be the best person I can possibly be by continually working on my flaws. That, I believe, is my life purpose. However, yours will be very different from mine. You might work twelve hours a day to support your family, sacrificing your time with them so they can have a better life, or maybe you spend all of your time assisting those in need, or maybe you are a teacher helping grow the minds of our youth, or maybe you own a small business that is providing a paycheck to others, or maybe you are protesting and standing up for something you believe in, or maybe you are a stay-at-home mom who is nurturing a beautiful little soul. I can literally go on and on about our different life purposes; nevertheless, I will let you determine that one on your own.

Eleven

Unveiling the Truth behind Our

Emotions and Our Guilty Feelings

The way we experience things is simply the display of our minds.

We all have a similar energy and a desire to feel loved. We are the only energies on planet Earth who are intellectually capable of articulating our feelings (that we know of). On top of that, we are also the only creatures who are able to experience so many different levels of emotions. Sadness, happiness, anger, remorse, love, and acceptance are a few of the common emotions we experience. Each emotion we are exposed to can be logically examined as a passing cycle. We tend to experience one of these emotions for a few moments; the next may be a few days or sometimes even years, but the reality is that normally these emotions are not long-lived. All these feelings can quickly subside as long as they are dealt with compassionately.

It is OK to experience sadness, hate, or whatever it might be. When we have an understanding that the emotional intensity will eventually pass, it is healthy to allow ourselves to feel these strong emotions. We should not be ashamed or pass judgment on ourselves for feeling any sort of way. We are human, and it is part of our human experience to feel our feelings. We should feel blessed to have all these different levels of source that we can connect to.

Some of the greatest poetry is written in sadness. In hate, we finally decide to stand up for ourselves. In love, we write music and in anxiousness that we grow.

When discussing "feeling our feelings," I am not suggesting that we act on our negative impulses but, rather, recognize that we have a choice to either surrender to it or observe it. And when we choose to observe it, we gain confidence knowing that we have the power to make decisions on how we choose to respond to the events impacting our lives. Simply acknowledging that we will eventually be faced with these uncomfortable experiences but knowing that we have the ability to control our reaction should help settle any discomfort.

As the Dalai Lama famously said (which was quoted by Thomas Bien in his *The Buddha's Way of Happiness*), "for anger, evoke love and compassion; for sadness, happiness; for agitation and worry, serenity; for envy, sympathetic joy." Although we might be feeling upset, science has proven that smiling will evoke more feelings of happiness. So if happiness is always available to us, we should embrace it. Our true nature is love and happiness, and when we become optimistic, our internal energies start to produce these euphoric feelings. Naturally inviting in what truly brings us joy. Another quote I am obsessed with states, "Happy people live in a world where good things occur all the time. Loving people see kindness everywhere. Curious people find life endlessly interesting" (Dalai Lama).

Overall, I have discovered that my bliss comes from finding happiness in others' successes. Helping others achieve what is important to them is what is most important to me. There is a term called "enlightened self-interest." This is a philosophy that basically means that you are deriving self-satisfaction from being kind to others. I personally find this to be an interesting notion. There is no doubt that we feel better about ourselves when we are making others feel better, but what about when we feel guilty that their situation is different than ours? Meaning, have you ever looked at a homeless person and thought to yourself, "Why did I get blessed with this life when they are struggling to find a warm place to sleep?" Or, have you ever felt ashamed for feeling upset about running out of coffee in the morning when there are millions of starving people in this world?

This type of suffering arises from our attachment to our beliefs. We have learned that we should feel guilty when someone else is not doing so great. This is deeply rooted in our past experiences. If as a child you were told to finish your meal because there are millions of starving people in the world, this could actually be an idea you have subconsciously grown attached to. The prohibiting thought pattern would be, "If I don't eat my meal, I should feel guilty that others are hungry." But when we actually look at this assumption, we come to realize that our guilt will not be solving any world hunger issues. However, if we choose to utilize this feeling of guilt in a more productive manner, we might be able to accomplish some good. For instance, when you see someone who is living on the streets and a feeling of guilt arises in you, maybe instead of holding on to that guilt, you could either offer to pay for their lunch or maybe you choose to volunteer at a local food bank. When our thought patterns become counterproductive, they are not benefiting anyone.

If we can establish an appreciation for those moments where we experience discomfort, we might be able to grasp a deeper understanding as to where those thoughts and emotions have stemmed from. In turn, having a greater understanding of our subconscious minds and why we react in certain ways helps us realize that these moments of suffering arise from attachment to our beliefs.

Just like an addict. Things need to get worse before they can ever get better. If we hit our rock bottom, we typically come to a realization that things now need to get better. Our subconscious mind becomes our conscious mind and screams at us, telling us that we deserve better for ourselves or that we need to be better for the people around us. Either way, this is a great motivator when accomplishing our goals.

Twelve

PERSONAL DEVELOPMENT

Change yourself, not others.

No matter how much we would like, we cannot change the past, nor can we change the future. Accepting that we must live with what has already passed and knowing that we have no control over the events to come help us understand the importance of living in the present moment. Coming to terms with our own impermanence can encourage an urgency for change. Every moment we get to spend with our family, friends, pets, and so forth is a precious one and should be treated that way. We must consider that we might not be blessed with the opportunity to spend time with our loved ones again. Every moment spent on this earth and with the ones we love should be recognized as a precious gift from God.

The Energy Bus by Jon Gordon sums up "personal development" perfectly in the following eight steps:

1. Remember that you are in control of your own life.
2. Surround yourself with positive-minded people.
3. Do not waste your energy on those who only have negative input.
4. Create your own future.

5. Trust that great things are happening.
6. Enthusiasm attracts more positive people into your life.
7. Love the ones around you.
8. Live purposefully.

Taking ownership allows us to take back our control. When we are blaming others for our issues, we allow them to be in control of our circumstances and the way we feel about those circumstances. But when we take ownership, we have the ability to make a positive change. So when we make positive changes in our life, we will naturally attract more positive people and more positive experiences. Remember that being happy is a choice. As the Buddha so eloquently stated, "There is no way to happiness, happiness is the way."

Happy people attract happy people, and the best gift we can give to anyone is being happy ourselves. The impact that happy people have on the world is obvious. Happiness is contagious, so when we surround ourselves with happy people, feelings of happiness naturally occur. Being present and deciding to choose happiness opens up our channel to the universe and allows us the opportunity to receive. When we choose to open up, live optimistically, and live in the present moment, we will receive endless solutions and opportunities. You just need to listen and allow it in. Just flow!

So when I say, "Open up to the universe, and you shall receive," that does not mean that you just sit back and wait for all the good to come. You must also make an effort to nurture your happiness. You can do this by setting good intentions and by planning a healthy lifestyle shift. If you know that, you function on a higher level after spending time in nature. Make it happen, and make it happen often. I personally believe that being in nature and spending time outside create happier people. Also, make sure to embrace your creative side more often. Find what feeds your soul and lifts you into a space of prolific joy.

Here is a small list of hobbies that might help you get started:

Blogging
Interior design

Flipping furniture
Yoga
Swimming
Hiking
Bike riding
Canoeing
Woodworking
Painting
Boating
ATV'ing
Camping
Music
Playing an instrument
Library
Volunteer work
Magic
Crafting
Baking
Sewing
Gardening
Couponing
Writing
Poetry
Photography
Church
Thrifting
Styling
Organizing
Coaching

Whatever it is, there are trillions of things that you can try. If you suck at it and it does not bring you joy, then move to the next thing. We cannot be good at everything, but we are definitely gifted in at least one thing. It will be trial and error, but once you connect with your creative passion, you will just know. For example, I have tried baking numerous times in hopes that my outcome will be better each time, but sadly it always turns out terrible. No matter what I make, it seems to take all day long. It stresses me out, and it drains all of my energy. Overall, I have learned that it is probably not my thing. However, when I indulge myself in a good self-help book or sit down and write for hours and hours, I feel connected to my soul, the world, and everyone around me. It is such an uplifting feeling. Just trust me; keep at it, and you will find what you love to do.

Deciding to make changes takes courage, planning, and commitment. Look at the elements in your life that are not conducive to your well-being and come up with a solution to change it. When you have identified what is making you unhappy and you can let go of the need to control others, you can then focus on the changes you need to make within yourself. For example, if you hate your job, it would not be wise to just walk away and quit. I am sure, like most people, you have bills to pay or a family to feed, but when you bring awareness that your job is creating unhappiness in your life, you can plan accordingly. Start off by casually looking on the internet for a new job, update your résumé, start telling this to friends and family members, or maybe take an online course. These few small things will start opening up doors to the world and to the universe, and before you know it, you will have opportunities knocking at your door. If you are clear on what needs changing, everything else will fall into place. Be brave and confident in your decisions. Without change, nothing will ever change.

Thirteen

WORKING WITH OUR EGO

Those who are subconsciously self-sabotaging are always making excuses completely ambivalent of their actions.

Our ego is truly an incredible powerhouse within our awareness. Our physical and mental well-being are greatly affected by what the mind believes. Just consider the placebo effect. When our physical or mental health can improve by taking a fake pill, it proves that our mind is an extremely powerful component within our bodies. We are what we think; however, not all thoughts are in the forefront of our awareness. Some of our prohibiting thoughts are within our subconscious mind. These are the thoughts that we really have to dig deep to heal. Yes, this can be a very scary process, but there are many professionals with the ability to safely assist you in uncovering these uncomfortable belief patterns.

But what exactly is the ego? The ego is an internal force that has been modified by our experiences. For instance, when I was a teenager, I lost two friends. One was murdered, and the other passed prematurely in a motorcycle accident. These two events had a profound impact on my life. As I grew older, I would still feel sad about these events, but they were not continually on my mind. So I thought . . . But during a challenging time in my life, when I was experiencing postpartum depression, I decided to see an acupuncturist that our marriage counselor had recommended. This acupuncturist specializes in a treatment known as NADA protocol/hypnopuncture, which I have personally found beneficial. However, I struggle to explain the process, so I would prefer to reference the benefits of NADA from her pamphlet.

NADA stands for National Acupuncture Detoxification Association, and what this treatment does is, it targets certain points in your ear that can help relieve stress and emotional trauma, reduce cravings, minimize withdrawal symptoms, help those who are struggling with anger and frustration, increase calmness, help you sleep better, and even give you a better sense of well-being. Our ears hold a microsystem (a very precise map) of the human body, the same map that exists in the cerebral cortex. Ultimately, ear acupuncture takes advantage of the body's own control center—the brain—where all these signals induced by the ear travel through to the corresponding body parts, triggering the body to systematically obey the commands, because they come from the brain.

Hypnopuncture is a combination of hypnosis and acupuncture. When we are in a hypnotic state, we enter our theta brain wave state, and in this state, we can access our subconscious mind by bypassing our critical thinking abilities.

So when NADA and hypnopuncture are combined in Natalie's seventy-minute session, our conscious mind logically and rationally wants to move us toward a solution. (If you are at all interested in her treatments (with her permission), I will add her contact at the end of this book.)

Now returning to my story. During my initial NADA/hypnopuncture session with Natalie, I was experiencing a profound level of depression. I am not sure that I actually recognized or admitted being in that state, but I did know that something was not right with me. I was crying a lot, I was easily triggered, and I had no desire to socialize. And if you knew me at all, you'd know that I was typically highly optimistic and loved engaging in conversations with others. During the session, she inserted approximately twenty or more needles, several of which were strategically placed on pressure points associated within my ears. She then used tuning forks to help align my Qi and find points in the body where my frequency was out of tune. She also used specific tuning forks to help balance the energy in those points. Then she started the hypnosis treatment on me. Here I set an intention that we would use for all six sessions. My intention was to find peace, calmness, and to be in tune with the world around me. We underwent the hypnosis process, and there I remained in a hypnotic meditation for forty to sixty minutes. This was the place that I could calmly listen to my ego/subconscious mind, and it was the most peaceful my mind had felt in a long time. Thoughts would calmly come and pass, and those that were in need of significant restructuring would stay with me until they felt resolved. I did not experience serious revelations until my second or third session, and in these sessions, I realized I was holding on to attached feelings regarding my friends who had passed (subconscious mind). I also realized that these attachments were affiliated with my fear of dying and leaving my family behind (the ego). Especially my kids. You have no idea how many times I would bawl my face off thinking about my own mortality. I could not bear the idea of not seeing or being with my children ever again, yet in this moment of hypnosis, it felt right to let these attachments go. Not necessarily leave them behind but to understand that they have served their purpose in helping me discover my spirituality and what exists after death. It helped me come to the realization that there is a healthy balance between living each moment as if it were the last and living in the past.

This process also helped me realign the energy in my body. If you know anything about postpartum depression, one would know that it is closely linked to hormonal imbalances. I literally had just given birth to a tiny little human who was growing in my body for the last nine months. Of course, this would change my biochemistry and affect my mood, my physical energy, and the way I was thinking. I just gave everything I had to allow this beautiful baby to thrive within me. In my personal opinion, this is the most miraculous example of our existence. Yet somehow, almost magically, the NADA/hypno-puncture sessions helped me rebalance my energy after only six treatments. Something that took me over two years to accomplish after my first two babies.

When we examine the thoughts within our ego, it is important to understand the correlating restrictive thought pattern. For instance, another revelation that I had was that I needed to spend more time with my mom. This thought came from within my subconscious mind, but the ego/restrictive thought pattern was "Why should I bother inviting my mom to our party when I know she will say no?" I will slightly dive into this thought. First off, my mom is one of the most generous people I know. She is a vigilante for those with no voice, extremely creative, independent, and kindhearted, and she has a deep appreciation for her animals. She took me in and let me live with her during one of the hardest times in my life and has a heart of gold. However, her life circumstances have made her very reclusive. She often makes comments such as "I hate people," "I prefer to be alone," "I don't go out in public."

Of course, during the pandemic, her reclusive behavior deepened. She suffers from multiple autoimmune disorders and made a choice to protect herself from the harm of COVID-19. Despite her choice of solitude, you would have no idea that she preferred to be alone. She is very outgoing in social settings, can talk to literally anyone, and people naturally gravitate to her outspoken personality. Amid the chaos of 2019–2022, my family and I chose to continue our social lives. We threw parties and had family gathering. We did what we would normally do, minus the limitations the government put on us for not being vaccinated. Please *note*: that I am non-bias and respect both sides of the spectrum when it comes to masking or not masking. Absolutely zero judgment here. In my opinion, we are all connected, and it is OK to have different views. Actually, it's what makes us interesting. Throughout the pandemic, my mom rejected many of our invites; she limited her contact to us, knowing that we were not being careful, and chose to keep herself safe. I highly respect this. We still communicated regularly, and she often visited the kids whenever she could. So when I dove into my subconscious mind and reflected on this thought of not including my mom, the story I was telling myself looked like this:

My restrictive thought pattern was:
   Why should I invite my mom when she will say no anyway?
   It won't bother her to not be included.

The reality:
   The pandemic had slowed down.
   It was rude to not include her even if she decided to say no.
   It was her choice to come or not.
   I wanted her to be there with us.
   And I missed my mom.

I feel like our ego and our subconscious mind are interconnected. The ego is the voice of the subconscious mind, and its primary job is to keep us safe. My interpretation of the ego is that it is there to distract us from what is actually troubling us. It is protecting us from feeling the emotions we might not be ready to face. The first step in dealing with deeply rooted emotional issues is to become aware of the obsession or the compulsion. Find out what it is that you might be reacting to and what you might be doing in order to avoid dealing with it. Analyze what behaviors your ego might be portraying to protect you from uncomfortable thoughts, and start by just recognizing that the thought or action is there. You will be surprised at how quickly you can correct these behaviors by simply acknowledging them.

Fourteen

Embracing Compassion and Understanding

Through love we release our judgements.

—Michael A. Singer (*The Untethered Soul*)

An important question to ask ourselves is "Why do I feel justified in making judgments toward others?" When we become highly critical of others, it is not the other we are actually criticizing; it is actually something within ourselves we are struggling to adapt to. So if I call Sally a spoiled *beep-beep* because she just got herself a new Porsche, it's not Sally who has the issue. It is me struggling with my jealous tendencies. So, rather than be happy for Sally, I react by telling myself the story that Sally is just a gold digger who sleeps around to get what she wants. However, there is absolutely no truth behind that statement, and it is highly overexaggerated. This is a very damaging and insensitive judgment that I am portraying toward Sally. So, when we have strong feelings of judgment, it is best to look within oneself to identify the insecurities directing these feelings. Like I mentioned with the ego. Once we start noticing these judgmental thoughts, they are more likely to reveal their truths.

Judging others is so embedded in our psyche that it is near impossible to imagine someone or something without judging them. For instance, when I think of the worst crimes committed against a child, I actually believe that I could torture and murder the person who had committed those crimes. Seriously. I personally believe that people like that do not deserve to walk the earth and should never be given a second chance. That judgment is deeply engrained in me, and I doubt I will ever let it go. But when I think of these feelings, I feel anger, and I feel anger because I feel helpless. So, it is also important to be kind to yourself when some of these judgmental feelings are evoked. If it were not for judgment, there would be no justice in the world.

However, we often judge people we do not even know for things that we are not even sure of. If we can bring awareness to the judgmental thought when it appears, we can more easily distinguish between the reality and fictitious elements of the story we were telling ourselves. Ask yourself questions such as "How does this judgment make me feel? Is there a moment from childhood that could be triggering this reaction? What and who am I judging and why? Is this judgment accurate, and is there any truth supporting it?" Looking deeper within your judgmental reactions might help you to identify a specific pattern emerging. And once this pattern has been identified, it will be easier to put a halt to the judgmental reaction.

Also, note that like everything else in life, this will take a lot of practice and patience. We are literally rewiring a behavior we have developed and been practicing since childhood. So be kind to yourself during this process and understand that removing these behaviors is not an easy process.

When a mother loves her child, she loves that child unconditionally. She loves her child more than herself, and although that child might engage in activities she disapproves of, she will still love her child with her whole heart. If we take this concept into consideration and then apply it to how we treat others, we can identify that we should allow people to be who they are without our judgments.

Michael A. Singer said it best in his book *The Untethered Soul* when he said, "When we can finally love every creature, every animal, every plant. When we can look at the dirt and appreciate the fact that without it, we wouldn't have beautiful trees or gorgeous flowers and then we truly love the dirt. When we love every child as if they were our own and when we can love others and appreciate the uniqueness they have to offer the universe, this is when we can release judgement."

Another way that we judge others is by having too many expectations of them. If we let go of our expectations of others, we will no longer be let down by them. No expectations, no letdowns. Now hear me out. Let us say it is your birthday, and you have been planning to celebrate it with your girlfriends (like you do every year), but this year when the day comes around, you do not get a phone call, not even a text message. You are extremely letdown and upset, and all these judgmental thoughts start intruding your brain: "How could they do this to me? How rude! They must all hate me!" and so forth. However, in reality, Rhonda was in the hospital, Karen was dealing with a lot of stress at work, and Donna was on a trip with her family. They did not intentionally forget your birthday, and there was nothing diabolical about it. They merely forgot.

Now let us say you were not expecting to celebrate your birthday. You were only happy to have turned thirty-six and were looking forward to spending a quiet night at home with your family. Now when anyone reaches out to wish you a great day, it is a bonus and you feel thrilled that they had thought of you. If not, no biggie. You did not expect it anyway. This is another example of living presently and will help to release judgments that grew from hurt feelings.

Rather than judging, we should try to evoke feelings of empathy. Try to see and feel the way others might feel. Also, try to understand that most situations are not intentionally callus. When we can love others and empathize with their situations, we can have a different understanding of the situation. In fact, when we empathize, we are more likely to have a more optimistic outlook on the situation. More importantly, we need to realize that we have no idea what someone else's situation might be. So, the next time you see that homeless person asking for change, maybe consider that their life's struggles were more challenging than your own. Just think about how hard it would be to stand on the street corner and ask for money. It would surely be a massive jab to anyone's pride, and I cannot imagine that they envisioned it for themselves.

Be kind. Love one another and be empathetic.

Fifteen

SURRENDERING CONTROL

*It is only when you're willing to experience things just the
way they are, that the level of unpleasant thoughts and
feelings finds a natural balance in the ecology of the psyche.*

I think it is safe to say that we have all had our struggles with control. Whether we are on the receiving end or dealing with our own self-control issues, we have all encountered some type of control at one point or another.

How many relationships have been ruined by our need to control the situation or having someone else force their controlling nature on us? Often this is the case in marriages and our careers. Once we get comfortable enough in a certain environment, it is easy to feel like we need to control everything revolving around it. Or, maybe we even have some sense of entitlement or expectations we think deserve to be met.

When we have this inner desire to have everything just so, it prevents us from being happy. I know a woman who gets worked up about a week before she hosts an event, has to go to a family outing, or is invited to a friend's house for coffee. She always focuses negatively on the amount of work she has prior to the event and stresses that her life is far too busy to engage in these types of outings. However, when the time comes to be present at the event, she always has a great time and is the life of the party. If she were to clearly look back at the stresses and the need to have everything perfect, I think she would agree that all the negative emotions were absolutely pointless. First off, she has been strung out for weeks, which would raise her cortisol levels and would likely affect her physical health. Second, stressing about every small detail from a negative perfectionist's standpoint is completely unnecessary. The obsession with uncertainty and the need to control everything within a situation is exhausting and takes a lot of effort. But what we need to recognize is that the future is uncertain. We will never have control over the outcome of our future. We can only pray for the best.

Being prepared is not controlling the situation. It is important to be organized and prepared for certain events, but that does not mean that we should manipulate and bend time to give us our desired outcome. In order to enjoy life and feel happy, we need to be open to "going with the flow." When we release our attachments to needing things a specific way, a huge weight can be lifted off our shoulders. Such as going on a road trip with your family. It is fine to plan where you will be camping ahead of time, prepping lunches, and having a few touristy spots to visit, but if your daughter wants to stop at the fresh fruit stand or your husband would rather take the scenic route, that is OK! Just flow with it! Be open to change. This is where you will truly discover what life has to offer. And in my personal experience, this is when the universe gives you exactly what you need. There are endless opportunities for discovery when you go off the beaten path and allow the universe to lead you where you need to go.

Acknowledging that life is uncertain and that things are bound to change can give us freedom from our controlling nature. Try to relax into these moments rather than resisting them. When you bring awareness to your resistance of change, you can help yourself adapt to a more spontaneous way of living. Bringing attention and simply looking at these feelings of control can help us come to realize that these thoughts and feelings are not as fixed as they may have originally appeared.

Life does not stay in place, not even for one second, and when we choose to cooperate with the inevitable, we become free. The most important thing is the thing we are doing now. Try to be totally invested in what is happening now. If you are coloring with your son, be fully present and fully committed to that moment. Let him do his coloring the way he wants to do his coloring, and just be there with him enjoying every second. Because this moment is the last moment that you will ever experience that moment.

Once you change your perspective toward the world, your whole experience shifts to a positive one. It is looking at getting stuck in traffic as an opportunity to finally relax and have some time to yourself. You realize you have no control regarding the pace of traffic and choose to look at the circumstance optimistically. It is when continually having to take your parents to the doctors but realizing that it is a great opportunity to spend quality time with them before they pass, knowing that their time here is limited. It is about seeing the upsets in life as an opportunity to grow as a person. You deserve to be happy, and this life is impermanent. We get one opportunity to be as great as we can be, so why not be happy and present while we are doing it?

Often we also try to control others and their behaviors. This is not our place. Each one of us is living a unique experience on this planet, and we all have the ability to choose how our life should be. We need to let go of our solutions to others' problems. What might be great for my life will not necessarily be great for someone else's life. If you see someone continually struggling with the same issues and all of your solutions are rejected, the only solution is to let go of your attachment to help and give her love instead. Send her loving thoughts, tell her she is loved and valued, be positive in her presence, and give more and more love. Be supportive and kind and offer advice, but do not expect it to be accepted. This is our duty as a human being. It is not to judge but to love and support one another.

I know it is often tough to sit back and watch the suffering of someone you care about, but through my experience, I have noticed that the other person must take control of their own life. They likely do not see the end of their own suffering as clear as we may. In turn, dismissing any advice and going about things on their own terms. Rightfully so, since what may have worked for us may not work in the same way for them. It is more important for us to give love and support but not our place to try and control the situation. Giving love is far more beneficial than advice.

However, it is important to set boundaries when dealing with other people's sufferings. If your aunt is a drug addict and running your bank account dry, you *need* to set boundaries. You can be clear with them that they have your love and support but that your wallet and your home are closed until they choose to get sober. As hard as setting boundaries might be since you are in fear of what might happen to them and have this need to control their safety, it is the best thing that you can do for yourself and for your loved one. Enabling them is just feeding your need to control their outcome and in turn is slowly killing them.

Ask yourself these questions when you feel the need to control a situation:

1. What am I afraid of if I let go?
2. Why does this scare me?
3. What is the likelihood of this situation ever happening?
4. Is my worrying about it going to change the outcome?
5. Is this stress beneficial to me?
6. Will worrying resolve the problem?

This is a prayer that I made for myself to help me overcome my issues with control:

Dear God, please help me learn to let go of control. Rather than try to predict future circumstances, please help me become present in the moment. Please help me appreciate the ones closest to me and help me stay focused on the positive aspects of my life rather than the negative. Please help me to understand that life is too short to stress over mediocre things such as chewing noises and heavy breathing. Instead, it is to be grateful for all the positive things that always outweigh the negative. Please remind me to let my loved ones know how much they mean to me, and please help me reconnect with my optimistic self. Please grant me the patience to deal with any challenges that may come my way and to be aware of the lessons attached in order to grow. Please help me discover my passions and grant me the courage to pursue them. Instead of fearing failure, help me see my mistakes as opportunities to become better. Please allow me to understand that I may encounter opposing opinions and to appreciate that their point of view is as important to them as mine is to me. Please help me become fully present, optimistic, loving, kind, patient, outgoing, passionate, friendly, grateful, and understanding. Please help me become better than yesterday.

Sixteen

PRACTICING SELF-LOVE

*If I am not for myself, who will be for me? And if I am
not for others, what am I? And if not now, when?*

—RABBI HILLEL

Self-love is such an important part in attaining peace and happiness. We might think that our inflated ego is defining our self-worth, but it is actually the opposite. When we have a false sense of our own image, we become fake and end up damaging who we truly are.

My whole life I was concerned with "title." I wanted to be known as an independent, financially successful woman who took care of herself. In hindsight, that sounds kind of fine, but when I chose a career as a mortgage broker to attain those goals, I realized that life is more than what others define you as. Life is about spending time with the ones you love, sharing meaningful conversations with others, sharing energy with one another, and discovering the beauty change can bring. When I quit brokering, quit my account management position, and became a contract laborer on a production line and started my own cleaning company, my life became way happier. It was a simpler position, but I was able to send my nine-year-old son off to school every morning, be home for him when he arrived back, cook healthier meals for my family, spend more quality time with my animals, go to yoga, work out, meet with friends more regularly, have vacation whenever I wanted, and still have the ability to pay all of my bills. I realized it is not about the title or about how much you earn; it is all about the quality of life that you keep.

I think that we all have this perspective that we are failing at life. But we are all doing the best we can, given our circumstances. Of course, there is always room for growth, especially when it comes to loving ourselves. If you were to ask someone close to you what they honestly thought of you, I think you would be pleasantly surprised by what they had to say.

The truth is that we need to forgive ourselves for our past mistakes before we can ever be freed from its restraints. In order to accomplish this, we need to empathize with our past and understand that we were not properly equipped with the tools or knowledge to handle whatever it was that we continually beat ourselves up for. We did the best we could, and now that we know differently, we can move on and do better for our future.

Every moment in our lives is valuable. When life is easy, there is no need to grow. And when our lives become purposeless and all our needs are met, we can lose our passion for everyday experiences. If we are left without the distractions of maintaining our basic needs, we are left with only ourselves and our thoughts. And if we do not like ourselves, this can be a difficult task to overcome.

Try to set a small amount of time aside each day to appreciate yourself. I would suggest starting every day with some uplifting affirmations. I personally write mine on my mirror with an erasable sharpie so that I do not forget to practice.

Start with affirmations around things that you might feel physically insecure about. For example, if you feel insecure about your eyelashes or eyebrows, use affirmations such as "My eyelashes look really full and thick today" or "Holy! I penciled my eyebrows perfectly today." Once you get into this habit, you will be surprised how your body and mind respond to these positive thoughts. Your eyelashes will grow thicker, your skin will be brighter, and overall you will begin to feel more confident and happy with your appearance. Your mind does not know the difference between an imagined thought and real one. So, when you continually affirm yourself with positive thought, your thoughts about yourself will also positively shift.

Clearly, self-love is not derived fully by how you feel about your physical self, but in order to love your whole self, you need to also feel confident with your physical self. That might mean changing up your routine throughout the day. Start off by waking up earlier, meditating, eating a healthy breakfast; take your vitamins, go to the gym, have a steam, take a hot or cold shower, and wear your favorite outfit. I guarantee you that if you can get into a routine like this at least five days a week, you will start feeling more confident, calm, and happier. Not only will you feel better about the way you look; you will start genuinely loving yourself more.

Some confidence-boosting affirmations such as "I am intelligent," "I am kind," "I have a good heart," "I am patient," "I keep a positive attitude," "I learn things easily," "I am creative," and "I am loved" are massive mood boosters. When you practice loving yourself, everything changes. Your relationships change, the people you draw into your life change, the way you choose to see the world changes. Trust me. It is worth trying. I mean, it is free and you deserve to be kinder to yourself.

When we discover how important it is to love ourselves, we begin to end our own suffering. We should praise ourselves and feel proud that we have overcome any misfortunes we have faced. Sequentially having improved as a human, we really need to give ourselves more credit. The more we have suffered, the more credit we should give ourselves. Those tragedies or hardships were not easy to overcome, and those moments of suffering have ultimately made us the best versions of ourselves. So we should feel grateful to ourselves for being strong and working through these issues.

We all have the ability to change, and I am proof of that. Although people often have perceived me as happy-go-lucky super positive person, I actually had a very dark side, and I had very, very low self-esteem. I was suffering from anxiety and depression and was extremely insecure. Although everyone who knew me likely would have described me as confident, positive, and cheerful, I felt the complete opposite inside. Why? Because I did not love myself, and I was always looking for confidence boosters through the approval of others.

When I was younger, I was a selfish troublemaker. I stole, lied, manipu-lated, and abused drugs and alcohol. But in some ways, I am grateful to have had been that person. If it was not for experiencing a lower level of being, I may have never discovered how to be a better person and truly honor myself. I now live my life in an honest, caring, empathetic nonjudgmental way. And I feel there is no other way to live my life. Through my troubling times, I learned that we are all connected and that love ends up being the answer for every problem. Letting go of my judgments toward others and myself has helped me realize that we are all only human and that this is part of our human experi-ence. No one is better than anyone else, and we can all learn from each other. Be kind to yourself, forgive easily, practice honesty, and release all judgments. This is how we can begin to truly love ourselves and others.

Seventeen

FREEDOM FROM RESENTMENT

A man can be imprisoned without chains
and a man can be free within chains.

—JEAN-JACQUES ROUSSEAU

When we hold on to resentment toward others, we are only punishing ourselves. Forgiveness allows us to be freed from that pain and suffering. If we choose to look at our situation differently, it might allow us to resonate with a different perspective. But it is not just others we need to forgive; we also need to forgive ourselves for the things we have done wrong.

If we dare to face the pain associated with the feeling of resentment, we can make one of two choices. We can choose to continue our feelings of resentment toward that person, or we can choose to forgive. If you prolong your feelings of resentment, you will be contributing to your own long-suffering—which means you will continue to feel angry, sad, tired, drained, and maybe even depressed. But when you choose to forgive, you have chosen a path of love. Your feelings are no longer running on a lower frequency, and you have advanced toward a path of healing.

Love is the only way we can break free of our chains. Whether it is someone else we are not forgiving or maybe it is ourselves, we are holding ourselves back from fulfilling our true potential. I am not saying forgiveness is an easy process. It is likely one of the most difficult processes you will ever experience emotionally. It is a choice that we make in order to free ourselves from the pain it has caused us.

In my past, I had experienced a lot of dishonesty within my more intimate relationships. At first, I turned a blind eye to the subtle cues, not realizing that the nonverbal signals I was receiving were massive red flags of infidelity. On and off, for approximately ten years, I experienced my lowest lows and faced my deepest insecurities. I was dealing with a broken heart and felt extremely jealous, insecure, and revengeful. I felt myself in this downward spiral. I tried to cope with drugs and alcohol. I turned to relationships that were very similar in nature, but not allowing anyone to get close enough to protect myself from the pain of feeling rejected again.

To make a very long story short, when I finally made the choice to move on from that relationship, my whole life changed. My mom was kind enough to take me in and help me get back on my feet, and her twin sister bought me a one-year gym membership to the local rec center. This is where my whole life shifted. When I started going to the gym and feeling better about myself, I then started attracting more like-minded people into my life, and I also discovered the healing world of self-help books. The first book I bought was called *The Buddha's Way of Happiness* by Thomas Bien, PhD forward by Lama Surya Das. I studied this book like crazy. It literally resonated with my soul. And when the book quoted "Change your perspective and your experience with change," I decided to do that exactly. I decided to forgive my ex and made a choice to stop hating all the women involved. I began to meditate on forgiving him and feeling empathy and sadness for him. Instead of hating him, I chose to be grateful to have him in my life. All this hate and resentment lifted from my shoulders, and I was finally freed from the shackles of anger. He was also free to start growing in a healthier, guilt-free way. We realized that God brought us together for many wonderful reasons and that all the suffering we endured as a couple was exactly what we needed to become better people. He now has a beautiful wife and a wonderful little family he loves more than anything. We both ended up getting what we wanted and needed out of the relationship, and I personally could not feel more grateful for the experience.

As Thomas Bien, so eloquently stated in his book, "Change your perspective and your experience will change," it allowed me to replace my feelings of resentment with feelings of compassion and gratitude.

We generally need to internally reflect to resolve our problems. The problem and answer always lies within. First off, we need to try to let go of any blame we might be holding on to. It will be difficult to come to a place of forgiveness when we are looking for an external resolution.

Through meditation, the answer should always come from the heart with love. And in this process, ask yourself important questions regarding the problem—for example, "Have I been honest in my relationships? What do I need out of a relationship to be happy or happier? Why do I feel so much hate toward this person? Is it possible that they might feel insecure, scared, or lost? What types of feelings can I evoke in order to help me forgive myself/others?"

This is your practice, so choose to fill your body with love. Be gentle, honest, and kind to yourself and those you are trying to forgive. Not all situations are easy to forgive, but I once saw this woman on a live courthouse show and rather than scold the young man who took her son's life, she told him she loved him and forgave him for what he had done. She hugged him and his mother and promised to help him through his struggles. If she could forgive this boy for taking her son's life in a hate crime, I believe it is possible to forgive almost anything, for forgiveness is giving you the peace of mind to move forward in a more positive way.

Eighteen

Welcoming Our Authentic Beauty

Our bodies are a reflection of our internal states.
For what we think of is what we become.

You already are what you inspire to be, so start treating yourself better. If you do not take care of yourself, you are incapable of taking care of anyone else. When we are constantly tending to the needs of others and not taking time for ourselves, we can become burned-out and bitter. And if we are burned-out, we are unable to be at our best for the ones who need us the most.

It is obviously important to take care of our daily duties and support the ones we care about, but it is equally important to take time for ourselves. I am not suggesting that you have to go on a lavish holiday, spend copious amounts of money on a new wardrobe, or treat yourself to regular spa days. What I am suggesting is that you start small. Maybe you are a stay-at-home mom, and all of your time and efforts are spent caring for your family. There are no breaks, time off, or wellness days. You are literally drained of all your energy and tending to the needs of others 24/7. So, why not start with something you can immediately control? Try waking up an hour before the kids do, enjoy a peaceful shower (with your favorite essential oil), get ready, start breakfast, and just enjoy your coffee in peace.

You can also do this in the evenings. Have your toddlers go to bed at a decent time, then sit on your patio with a hot cup of tea and enjoy the stars. The more time you are able to spend outside, the better you will feel inside. Fresh air is something people are lacking nowadays, and being in nature or just enjoying the flowers in your yard is such a soothing recharge. We as humans are meant to be outside, connecting with the earth. We should not be sitting in front of our laptops or TVs draining ourselves of the only energy we have left. A good amount of earthing has been proven to strengthen your immunity, lower blood pressure, and boost your mood. So why not power yourself up through something that is always readily available and free?

Or, instead of watching TV or scrolling the interweb, perhaps you could go to bed twenty minutes earlier for a nighttime meditation. There are thousands of guided meditations online and many apps that can help assist you in calming down. Meditating regularity can help decrease stress, improve your memory, elevate anxiety and contribute to healthier sleep patterns. Try to incorporate at least ten to twenty minutes of meditation each day. I promise, you will experience a positive difference within your mood and outlook on life.

Another way to make time for yourself would be by scheduling a daily-workout routine. Whether it is basketball, yoga, karate, boxing, or cardio classes, you will not only feel better but also you will notice a change in your physical appearance. You will begin to like the way your body looks and feels, and as a result, you will feel more confident and happy with yourself. My husband has literally woken up at 5:00 a.m. every day to go to the gym so that it does not conflict with his time at work or with our kids. Going to the gym and focusing our energy into an intense workout is the best way to rid the body of anxious feelings. But make sure you sweat. There is no point in going to the gym or a workout class if you are not willing to put in the effort. Start by doing ten minutes on a low-impact bike, then eventually try working your way up to a higher-intensity elliptical and then to a jog. Continue to increase your time and the level of intensity and you will notice a massive difference in your external appearance. You will even start feeling better internally. Adding physical activities to your daily routine takes a lot of discipline. But I guarantee you, once you practice this routine at least four to five days a week, it will be like having your morning coffee. You will always make it work and you will be extremely pleased with the results.

However, in order to feel your very best, you must also make healthier choices. When it comes to your diet, the solution to looking good and feeling better is actually simpler than you might think. When we start small and gradually work our way up, the mental impact of our choices are far more discrete. Substituting one slice of bread in the morning for an avocado or making a protein smoothie instead of eating all that chocolate in the cupboard will have a huge impact on your waistline. Try swapping your latte for a double shot of espresso, or start making larger portions at dinnertime so that you can pack the extras in your lunch. If your drink of choice is filled with sugars, opt instead for a sugar-free, low-calorie vodka soda. These might seem like small alterations to your diet, but once you get comfortable with your healthier food choices, you will naturally start gravitating to a healthier way of eating. We are what we eat, so try to choose more organic, natural foods when shopping at the grocery, and make sure you always have a healthy snack on hand. It is not worth making poor food decisions, because you were underprepared. Food fuels our bodies, so keep your tank full by eating smaller portions more regularly.

As RuPaul once said, "You're beautiful, you are strong, and it's worth taking care of yourself." So stop sitting on that couch feeling sad for yourself. You deserve to get out there and live a happy life. Pamper yourself and treat your body with kindness. If you add a personal hygiene routine, healthy sleep patterns, daily physical activity, plenty of outdoor time, a healthy diet, and meditate for at least ten minutes a day, you will feel incredible about yourself. Sometimes if my days are stretched for time, I will combine some of these activities. Such as adding a guided walking meditation while I take my dog out, or I will listen to a self-help book while running on the treadmill. I cannot say it enough. You deserve to love who you are, so put the effort in and commit to changing the way you feel about yourself. You are worthy of taking an hour or two a day for yourself, and you owe it to yourself and the people around you. The happier and healthier you feel, the happier the people around you will feel.

Nineteen

SELF-CONTROL IN TERMS OF DRUGS, ALCOHOL,

AND PRESCRIPTION MEDICATIONS

*Be strong enough to let go and wise enough
to wait for what you deserve.*

I personally believe that everyone has the opportunity before their last breath to make a change in their lives. Coping with drug, alcohol, or prescription medications can be a very difficult challenge to overcome. However, it is possible. One of the most influential people in my life has been sober for over thirty-five years and has never regretted one moment of it. Becoming sober and facing reality will be the best decision you ever make.

Drugs, alcohol, and prescription addictions can be an extremely damaging path and will not be easy to overcome. Actually, as I am writing this chapter, I myself am struggling with something that I will call "postpartum alcoholism." Postpartum alcoholism to me is drinking regularly to cope with the stresses that come along with parenting. Currently I have three children—aged fourteen, four, and two. They are literally my whole world, and I love them all to pieces, I could not imagine my life without them. I feel blessed and grateful to have these beautiful little humans in my life. But as soon as things in my household get a bit tense, I immediately reach for a vodka soda cooler or a glass of red wine. To most people, that might be considered fine, but I cannot stop at just one and find myself having anywhere from 2 to 4 drinks every night. When you do the math, that could potentially be anywhere from 60 to 120 drinks a month.

I tell myself that it relaxes me and that I am more fun and a better parent after a few drinks. Although in all reality, it affects my sleep and my mood and makes me feel depressed and ashamed of myself. There is no doubt that it has helped me cope with the stresses associated with the ups and downs of parenting small children, but in the process, I am damaging my mental and physical health with this socially accepted poison. Not only that, I am silently telling my children that this is the appropriate way to cope with negative or stressful emotions. I already notice my youngest ones grabbing juice boxes out of the fridge when mama is having a cooler. Why? Because they look up to me and want to be like me. And in my mind, this is completely unacceptable. I should be leading by example and making healthier choices. Not only for them but also for myself.

So, although I have been sitting here preaching about how to become happier and healthier, I have decided to take my own advice. From today, on September 18, 2023 (just days before my 38th birthday), I will start living a sober life. No more alcohol! Plain and simple.

The honest truth is that I have struggled with addiction my whole life. Pretty much from the age of twelve, I have been coping with life through alcohol, drugs, hallucinogenics, and lustful relationships. There have been many instances where I had successfully stopped drinking and was able to make a positive shift in my life, but I always seem to fall back into using alcohol to elevate the stressful moments in my life. I have, however, been able to overcome and permanently quit the drugs and lustful distractions with the help of the following steps.

In the book *The Buddha's Way of Happiness*, it suggests that in order to quit a habit energy, we should not struggle against the urge but instead allow the habit to pass naturally, having the confidence in knowing that through mind-fulness, it will pass naturally.

1. What is your reason to quit?
2. Practice delaying the craving.
3. Realize that habit energy is temporary and short-lived.
4. Sobriety sampling.
5. Find an alternative.

Personalize the aforementioned list. I am also going to do the same. Please see my following example:

1. My reason to quit drinking is for my kids and my own well-being.
2. I will practice delaying my cravings by having a piece of chocolate and slamming a glass of water instead. Also, finding a healthier zero-alcohol substitute.
3. I realize that habitual energy is only temporary and with strong will and practice, I will be able to overcome the urge to indulge.
4. When I am sober, I feel more energetic, happier, and proud of myself.
5. When I feel like drinking, I will instead reach for a bubbled ice-cold lemon water, or a hot tea, or maybe even a nighttime coffee.

I myself have never had issues with prescription drug medications, but I can see how they can easily become addictive. When I was nineteen, I was pre-scribed Percocet and T3s after breaking my collarbone. I was told to take two/day for pain management, and I did as I was told. The first two weeks of my injury are a total blur. I was highly medicated and living my life in la-la land. After polishing off my first round of medications, I made a choice *not* to refill the prescription due to my immediate dependence on it. Although I was still suffering with the pain, I knew that if I were to refill that prescription, I would become fully dependent on it.

There are many drug-free remedies such as psychotherapy, physiotherapy, acupuncture, group meetings, and natural supplements that can help alleviate pain and cravings. Quoted from the book *The Brain Fog Fix*, written by Dr. Mike Dow, "From a financial point of view psychotherapy is far more expensive in the short term than paying for your generic depression medications. While the effects of six months of cognitive behavioral therapy can last a lifetime, the antidepressant effects of Prozac stop when you stop taking them." Psychotherapy can be beneficial for all types of addictions and will have long-term effects.

What I believe Dr. Mike Dow is trying to say here is that it may seem more expensive now to enlist in psychotherapy treatment, but your anxiety medicines will end up costing you more in the long run. However, when it comes to any sort of addiction, I highly recommend seeking professional help. So, when you make that choice to face reality and commit to a wellness program, it helps you become emotionally committed to the process. Hence, why I decided to tell my story in this chapter. I needed to be committed to my word and hold accountable for my decisions.

Our bodies and our brains are so incredibly fascinating. Like I have said in previous chapters, "we are what we think," and there has been neurological studies claiming that everything that is available within a pharmacy is also available within our bodies. We just need to learn to tap in to the healing process. I believe we can attain this natural way of healing through the practice of meditation. I have heard of people who were told that they were paralyzed and would never be able to walk again. Yet over time and with an incredibly determined mindset, they were able to overcome their medical diagnosis by focusing on the inner workings of their body, sending positive energy and watching their nerves literally repair themselves through some sort of visionary healing process. This has literally happened time and time again. There are plenty of stories out there proving that the human body and mind are capable of miracles.

So, if the mind and body is this powerful, we should have faith that we can overcome anything in this lifetime. With the combination of determination, commitment, and the help of a naturopath or medical professional, we can start living our best life. When we choose to become sober, we have the opportunity to experience a greater spiritual connection with ourselves and the ones around us. We do not need alcohol or drugs to uplift us. As you know, short-term effects are more damaging in the long run.

When we contribute a solid effort and do things to the best of our abilities, I can guarantee you will feel satisfied with the results. Rather than turning to drugs or alcohol when we become upset, choose instead to go to your happy place. For example, when I am feeling overwhelmed with the chaos in my household, I will take fifteen minutes alone in my bedroom to practice Duolingo. This helps distract me from my negative energy and helps pull me away from the emotions attached to the situation. *Lo recomiendo.*

And if you are a parent of young children, I would strongly recommend spending as much time outside as possible. Nature is medicine. Surfing is medicine. Skiing is medicine. Hiking is medicine. Biking is medicine. Blading is medicine. Skating is medicine. Camping is medicine. Baseball is medicine. Hopefully, you get the point. The electrical properties of the earth are a natural source of medicine. Not only is being outside great for your kids, but also it is healing to your own soul. The earth's surface is full of free electrons, so roll around in the grass or jump in the river and absorb all that free healing medicine. I mean, it is free. Why not give it a try?

Twenty

OUR SMALL PERSPECTIVE

*To some, it is easy to get caught up and lost within
the monotony of our lives, continually living
through our days as though we are on repeat, really
neglecting the reality of what exists around us.*

Did you know that there are 8.7 million different species, 40–100 million different planets that are habitable within our own solar system? So why can't there be other intelligent life out there? Many people think that this claim will discredit the Bible and other religions, creating absolute chaos within our society. But in my personal opinion, it would only help make sense of the supernatural claims written by our ancestors. For instance, have you ever read *Chariots of the Gods?*

It suggests that the gods visiting us from the sky may have been extraterrestrial in nature. Maybe the very gods that we are worshiping are extraterrestrials. And did you know that scientists have found something like fifty thousand genes within an octopus's gnome. If we compare that with that of a human, which has twenty-five thousand genes, this would suggest that an octopus is far more complex than a human and theorists suggest that this complexity might come from outside. Maybe even outside of our universe.

I have had many unexplained experiences that have led me to believe that there is intelligent life outside of our planet. And it is highly likely that they are far more advanced than we are. I know this can be a huge hit to our ego, but when you look at what science has proven to date, it seems pretty darn likely that there has to be other habitable planets sustaining some sort of intelligent life.

There are four hundred billion stars in our galaxy, which means that there are likely four hundred billion planets in our galaxy. And recent estimates tell us that there could be as many as two trillion galaxies in the observable universe. How could we possibly not believe that there are other habitable planets in our galaxy?

There is no doubt that there is more to our existence than we might want to believe. Personally, I believe that our universal consciousness is expanding and humanity is finally realizing our capabilities of connecting through our consciousness. We are high-frequency beings; when we allow ourselves to tune in to different frequencies, we allow ourselves to experience different realities.

What I mean by this is that in my opinion, we are all connected through energy. Some of us are naturally in tune to this, and some of us need to work harder to tune in to this. However, we all have the ability to connect with one another through our energy. Whether this be on earth or outside of earth.

For instance, I can literally feel others' emotions as though they are my own. When I was younger, I had a hard time regulating these feelings, and as I said in previous chapters, I coped with these feelings through drug and alcohol abuse. I had no idea that these emotions were not mine, and I was not equipped with the right tools to handle the stress.

I actually did not realize how strongly I took on others' emotions until I had my experience with ayahuasca. I do believe this was a calling from the universe. Shortly after this calling, I found myself at a three-day retreat in the woods (by myself) trying to find a deeper connection with spirit. But what I found instead was how closed off I was to the group. Trying not to absorb all the negative energies coming from the traumas of everyone else's experiences, I took my dose, put in my earplugs, and curled up in the corner alone. I honestly do not remember a whole lot other than hating the experience. Purging was not pleasant, and it is not an experience I would ever recommend to anyone else, although I have had friends overcome serious addictions through these retreats. For me, this was the moment (in my early thirties) that I realized that I take on the emotions of others.

Although I have been learning to hold up boundaries since this experience. There is a connection that we all share in order to help us feel complete, especially when it comes to sharing positive energies with one another. We really need to disconnect to our fear of engaging with one another so that we can start lifting each other up and start sharing all the smiles and good vibes we have to offer. There is a reason why our grandparents' generation felt happier and overall more satisfied with their well-being. And there is a reason why our generation feels anxious most of the time. It is because we are tuned out and no longer connecting with people on a physical level. Although there are far more ways of connecting through technology, it is less natural and does not appease our mutual reciprocity. We need each other more than ever, and a smile will go a very long way. :)

Twenty-One

Nurturing Intimate Connections

*Real love is the intention to understand and go
on understanding even when it is difficult.*

To desire love and connection with a soulmate is, in essence, our sole purpose. I read somewhere that real love is the willingness to admit fault, to pick up ourselves and our partner, to forgive and be patient, but understanding that it will not be easy. And this really resonates with me. Being someone who was addicted to lust and the rush that came along with it, it was my belief that love should flow effortlessly and there should always be a feeling of excitement and desire. You know that feeling of pure ecstasy when you first start dating someone? You cannot wait to see each other; you are constantly dreaming of that person, you believe they are the greatest thing on earth, and the physical attraction is almost unbearable. Those were all the feelings that I felt when I first met my husband, but unlike the others, when those feelings subsided and we came down from the high, we were both willing to put the work in to make our relationship work. True love is about finding someone who makes you feel all the feelings, but once the euphoria of the relationship wears out, you continue to have faith in each other.

I was once fooled in to believing that love was jealous, controlling, obsessive, and challenging. But once freed of the controlling nature of being jealous,

I realized that love is equanimity, genuine compassion, nonjudgmental, and understanding. It is an unreal mental and physical phenomenon that releases our egotistical obsessions and allows us to be present with one another as is.

This does not mean that creating a genuine connection with someone is easy. It is actually the complete opposite. It takes a lot of hard work, forgiveness, adaptability, and flexibility. Finding the right partner is not an easy task, especially in this day and age where our digital dating menu keeps becoming larger and larger. Fortunately, this can also benefit us if we have a warm loving relationship with ourselves and have a general idea of the characteristics our ideal partner might possess. Of course, you might have a preference in the way your future partner looks, but mutual trust, emotional maturity, and compromise are the foundation to creating a healthy relationship.

Once you have found your soulmate, it is valuable insight to cultivate acceptance in knowing that all relationships are perfectly imperfect. Not every day will be a good day. Knowing how to let go of control and adapt to new and uncomfortable situations can greatly define our level of happiness with our partner. It starts with loving yourself first and knowing roughly what you want out of your relationship.

On the other hand, if you are feeling like your relationship is no longer serving you, it might be time to move forward and make some changes. It is important to understand that we are incapable of changing anyone else, and if you are feeling insecure or attached, it might be time to do some serious soul-searching to regain your confidence.

Keep in mind that the right partner will always be there to support you, make you feel secure, and will lift you up when you are down. Here are some questions to ask yourself if you are questioning the status of your current relationship.

Start off by being honest with yourself and with your relationships.

1. Are you happy in the relationship you are in currently?
2. Are the moments you share together uplifting and fun?

3. Or, are you finding that the majority of your time spent together are spent arguing or disagreeing?
4. What is it that you require from your relationship in order to feel fulfilled?
5. Do you need someone who is encouraging, genuinely enthusiastic, or exciting?
6. Is one giving more to the relationship than the other?
7. Is your partner worth the work?
8. And are you willing to accept the flaws of your partner in order to have a peaceful relationship?
9. Are you willing to make changes to yourself?

After reviewing these questions, you should have a better understanding of what you need to do. If you choose to move on, do it amicably and smart. If you are in a situation where you are concerned about your partner's reaction, make sure you are fully prepared to deal with the absolute worst. Play it smart. Especially if your children are involved. Make sure you make preparations to keep you and your children safe, and make sure you connect with family and friends to help you through what can be a very difficult and challenging time. Your family and friends will love, support, and keep you safe. And they will want to help you and your children if you are not in a safe place.

On the other hand, if you choose that your partner is worth the work, I would suggest finding a great marriage counselor. I highly, highly recommend "The Love of Attraction" course hosted by my marriage counselor, Kathleen Maiman. This is for couples struggling to overcome their negative funk. My husband and I did this weekend retreat in Banff Alberta back in 2023, and it was incredibly transformative for us. We gained a stronger understanding of each other's needs and greatly benefited from her Imago dialogue, which we continue to utilize in order to strengthen our connection. This course is also filled with all sorts of helpful techniques to help deepen your connection and communication skills with your children and partner.

When you decide this is the right person for you and you are willing to make changes, start by taking responsibility for your own actions. If you are constantly screaming and yelling, that needs to stop immediately. Apparently, most people scream and yell because they are not feeling heard. Find a way to communicate with your partner in a different way. Our counselor gave us an "Imago dialogue," which allows one person to amicably voice their concern while the other mirrors and validates their feelings—which allows both parties to feel heard. It is a fantastic way to communicate with one another, and it saves you from the exhausting screaming and yelling matches.

It is also very important to express your appreciation for one another. Let them know how much you care for them, and learn how to speak their love language. Maybe it is through physical touch or acts of service. Our actions mean a lot, but words coming from the heart can mean just as much or more. Show your gratitude to your partner and share twenty-seconds hugs when you are feeling overwhelmed.

And if you are looking for a new partner, be clear with yourself what you want out of a relationship. Make a written list of all your wants. What would they look like? Would they be funny? Would they be affectionate? Would you want them to have their own kids? Do you even want kids? What would be the physical things that would attract you to them? Where would they live in proximity to you? Should they like to travel? Should they be social? Should they be sober? Should they be serious in nature? What is your love language? and so forth. Once you have created a list of your perfect partner, cross off the things you would be willing to compromise with and leave the things that you will stand firm with. I made this exact list when manifesting my partner, and guess what? He showed up. Almost to a tee. Seriously!

If you look back at your relationship history, you might also recognize a pattern. Like, maybe you are continually attracting a similar personality that is not compatible with yours. If so, I would suggest choosing a better place and a different tactic to look for love. Personally, I was constantly attracting men with a wandering eye. Literally starting from grade school, every boyfriend I had was either interested in someone else or was with someone else while they were with me. It was not until my late twenties that I realized I needed to change the way I met men. I was clearly naturally attracting every douchebag out there, so I decided to try something different. Rather than accepting dates on the fly, I decided to try online dating, <u>match.com</u> to be exact. And through that site, it evaluated my wants and needs and matched me with numerous people. One of those men turned out to be the love of my life, my husband and the father/stepdad to my children. To this day, I am so grateful that I was courageous enough to try something different. Other than my brothers and my father, he is the greatest man I have ever met. He is loving, kind, hard-working, supportive. He is a great father and stepfather, and no matter how crazy I get, he always stands by my side. I feel blessed every day to have found someone as great as he is.

Having differences in a relationship does not mean that you are not meant for each other. It means that you are meant to learn from each other. My partner and I could not be more opposites. I am incredibly emotional; he is not. He can be very serious; I am not. I can be very frivolous; he is very frugal. But to be honest, this is what we both needed from a relationship. We needed to find a middle ground and balance. We need each other, and although we are completely different, there is this beautiful balance that we have discovered because of each other. It has been the most wonderful experience, and I am so grateful for everything he has taught me. And like our therapist always says, "You get what you need, not what you want."

Twenty-Two

FINDING HAPPINESS FROM WITHIN

*To embark on the journey to happiness, one
must first find the place within.*

We all have this common goal of wanting to attain happiness. It actually seems like it is our sole purpose to make this dream come true. And no matter who we are, where we come from, or what nationality we are, we all want the same thing. Happiness!

In order to obtain happiness, we first need to come to terms with the things that have been upsetting us. Have you been obsessing on some past event that is filling your brain with negative thought? If so, I would suggest trying to come to terms with the fact that there is no changing what has already occurred. Try to accept that what has already happened, has happened. Once you have chosen to accept it rather than suppress it, you can finally free yourself of its attachment. By accepting the fact that this is a reality you no longer have control of, you are in turn freeing yourself from its grasp on you.

There is no doubt that there are some events that are so incredibly traumatic that they will be more difficult to overcome. In this case, I highly suggest reaching out to a professional who can assist you in overcoming these traumas. It might be expensive, but your mental well-being is worth it. Try looking at it as an investment in yourself. We constantly spend hundreds of dollars each month on our nails, eyelashes, hair, booze, coffee, lips, and so forth; why not choose to invest this dinero into your mental health instead? This is a treatment where the benefits are long-term and long-lasting.

As Joseph Campbell eloquently conveyed in his poem:

Follow your bliss.
If you do follow your bliss,
you put yourself on a kind of track
that has been there all the while waiting for you,
and the life you ought to be living
is the one you are living.
When you can see that,
you begin to meet people
who are in the field of your bliss,
and they open the doors to you.
I say, follow your bliss and don't be afraid,
and doors will open
where you didn't know they were going to be.
If you follow your bliss,
doors will open for you that wouldn't have opened for anyone else.

I absolutely love this poem. There is so much truth written in his words. When we choose to open up to new experiences, we allow happiness into our world. When we try to resist the reality of what exists, we invite anger and hostility into our lives. For example, I booked a last-minute solo, all-inclusive vacation to Mexico. Due to bad weather, my flight was delayed almost five hours, but this did not bother me. I was just happy they did not risk the travel and made sure our plane was de-iced and safe before liftoff. However, when I finally arrived at my all-inclusive resort, it was pitch-dark, no one spoke English, the lock, phone, and TV did not work in my room, and I was furious. Not only did I just travel for ten hours, but also the resort was not your typical all-American, all-inclusive that I was expecting. No booze in the fridge, no bottled water, and so forth. I was furious to say the least. Before allowing some time to experience the resort and feeling somewhat entitled to a different experience, I called the travel agency and demanded new accommodations. I was literally having an anxiety attack. I was feeling nervous and uncomfortable, especially since my room door would not lock properly and I was all alone. I ended up spending hours on the phone with reps who were not accommodating at all, and in the end, nothing had changed. Frustrated and angry, I decided to barricade my door with chairs and go to bed for the night. In the morning, I decided to change my perspective and chose to give this place a chance. To my surprise, the resort was completely different than I had imagined the night before. Yes, it was completely different than your all-American Mexico all-inclusive, but it was so much more authentic and different than what I had experienced on past trips. The locals traveled here for holidays with their families, and despite the language barrier, everyone was so kind and always greeted me in passing. The hotel staff was incredibly helpful. They upgraded my room to make me feel more comfortable, and the food was truly authentic and absolutely delicious, none of this gluttonous all-you-can-eat stuff. This trip turned out to be a great opportunity to learn and adapt to a new culture. The experience will be one that I will never forget and will always be grateful for.

I think the lesson here was, when we have certain expectations, we end up setting ourselves up for disappointment. But once we choose to let go of our resistance, we no longer need to struggle with the idea of everything needing to be perfect in order to feel happy.

We have a choice to be happy, regardless of our circumstances. When we choose to look at every experience as an opportunity to try something new, we come to realize that happiness is everywhere. When I sat on that beach in Mexico and observed all the families enjoying their vacation, I noticed how connected they were with one another. They included the children, grandparents, sisters, brothers, aunts, and uncles. They took care of their elders, helping them find shade, while the older kids took care of the younger kids. There was a completely different culture and level of calmness, happiness, and contentment I was witnessing. Very different from my own culture, where it seemed to revolve around constantly being anxious and stressed out about the worst-case scenario. The Mexican women, no matter what size or shape, were stunning and nurturing, all radiating a magnificent confidence. Their holiday did not revolve around getting hammered and buying copious amounts of souvenirs. It revolved around the connection with their family, plenty of laughs, and playful energy.

Happiness is available to all of us, all the time. We should try to confront each situation with the aim to accept each circumstance. If we do not force our desired outcome and accept what it is, we will open ourselves up to a more optimistic experience. We have a choice to look at each situation as an individual experience, and we have the choice to respond optimistically.

Happiness comes from the heart and an inner knowing that you deserve to be happy. Happiness spreads from one to another, so even if you cannot be happy for yourself, start by being happy and optimistic for the ones around you. Even if you are faking it, it will eventually feel natural and authentic, especially if you put the hard work in to tackle your unsettling emotions.

To be truly happy is to let go of the idea of perfection. Perfection creates a feeling of being unsatisfied with ourselves all the time. Our quirks and our differences are what make us unique. When you can accept yourself and your situations as they are, life becomes far more exciting and fun.

The next step to becoming happy is to surround yourself with happy people. Maybe you are fortunate enough to have a great, fun-loving family. If so, choose to spend more time connecting and laughing with them. If not, create a family that you can rely on and that will pick you up with laughter. Sadly, we are not all blessed to have been born into a family of incredible people. But that does not mean you are obligated to spend your time with them. If they are not accepting of who you are, that is their problem. Instead, choose to surround yourself with people who love you for who you are; people who make you laugh; people you can share a deep connection with; people who are optimistic and wise; and, most of all, people who will stand by your side no matter what.

Everyone's version of happiness is different. Mine is writing and laughing with my family. My son's is on the basketball court, my daughters are the happiest when we are playing outside, and my husband's is on a boat on a sunny day catching fish. We are all different, and we will all experience happiness in different ways. Just remember, money cannot buy you happiness. It can get you what you desire in life, but if you are not already happy, your newfound wealth will only create more problems for you.

Being able to adapt to different situations will greatly improve your level of happiness. So, the next time you find yourself acting out after not getting what you want, try to remember: You can either choose to adapt and feel much happier with your situation, or can resist what already exists and create frustration for yourself and the others around you. Choose happiness instead.

Twenty-Three

RESTORING FAITH IN THE GOODNESS OF HUMANITY

Every day miracles will naturally occur once you
choose to have faith in the universal law.

—NIKKI WEBER

It is important in these times of terror and uncertainty to come together. Panic creates a false sense of security and selfishness. This type of energy can be extremely scary and contagious. And it is in these times that we need to help one another. For this is the only way we can guarantee our survival. Therefore, using kind words, being generous, and choosing to help wherever you can are the things that will renew humanity.

When we create community and take care of our neighbors, we will come to realize that we all need each other. Practicing compassion and empathy and choosing to share our good fortunes with others will help to support and grow our communities, giving us a sense of connectedness.

Random acts of kindness will go a very long way. Open the door for someone, or go out of your way to return someone's wallet. Visit your grandma for God's sake. Mow the elderly neighbors' grass, or better yet make sure their sidewalk is always shoveled in the winter. Offer your help to a family member with a project they are completing. Or, go out of your way to comfort a stranger who is clearly distressed. We are all very alike, and we need to take care of each other. How good would it feel if someone acknowledged you while you were down? I know that the acknowledgment alone would lift me up.

Be kind with your words, and try your best to lift each other up. Focus on the positive things about life and tune out the negative. Fight for what you believe in, and try to make a positive difference in the world. What you give, you will get back. So be generous whenever you can.

I was completely taken back when I went to purchase a product from a girl on Facebook. For whatever reason, my e-transfer did not seem to be going through. Rather than sit in my car and wait, she invited me in for a coffee. A complete stranger. We had so much in common and had a great conversation. I was completely shocked by her generosity and was incredibly grateful for her thoughtfulness.

Obviously, we need to proceed with caution when it comes to these acts of generosity. I watch far too much dateline to trust everybody. But I do like to think that most people are kindhearted and live with good intention.

And if you ever need a serious pick-me-up, I suggest watching queer eye. They are honestly so transformative, uplifting, and funny. I swear I laugh so much every time I watch this series, and I always shed tears at the end. I love how they not only transform people from the outside but also from the inside. It really truly is a beautiful thing. And they are sharing an incredible message with the world.

We do not have to be famous or have a TV show in order to do these type of good-natured things. We should make people feel great all the time. Especially the little people we are molding into adults. Put the dishes aside and go play dollies.

Twenty-Four

RETHINKING OUR VALUES

*We need to live our lives in a voluntary simplicity where we
find sincerity and honesty within as well as an avoidance
of exterior clutter of the many possessions irrelevant
to the chief purpose of life. Ordering and guiding our
energies and our desires to find our true purpose.*

—DUANE ELGIN

Nowadays, the world is focused on abundance and target marketing.
Not often will you find a product of high quality that will last generations to come. Marketing focuses solely on disposable products that are
specifically designed not to last. This is intentional! So that we as consumers
will continually be purchasing their products.

Today, marketing is focused on a maximum profit versus maximum use-
fulness, which has created the disposable society we live in today. The message
is . . . you are not pretty enough, your clothes are not nice enough, your lips
are not big enough, your washing machine is crap, these pots and pans will
make your food taste bitter, your skin is too oily, you do not have enough toys,
alcohol will bring you more friends and allow you to have more fun . . . yada

yada. Basically the message is, you need this to improve your life. So buy, buy, buy!

So why is it that we constantly fall victim to these messages? It is because we do not think we are good enough and that these products will bring us more happiness. However, as Thomas Bien stated in his book, "It is not the material things in our life that matter. Since we are matter and we will eventually die, these things will become meaningless. It is our good deeds that will carry our energy in to the future after death." With this statement in mind, we should not derive our worth through material objects; it should be through our acts of service and how we give back to our community. After death, your family and friends will not be honoring you for your stuff. They will be honoring you for the good deeds you have done and celebrating who you were as a person along with all the contributions you had made to your community. Rather than focusing all of our energy into monetary items, we should redirect our energy into giving back.

For many years I had struggled with the idea of accepting my financial situation, trying to portray an image that was literally imagined. But when I finally came to accept how blessed I was, no matter how rich or poor, I felt free to be myself. Who cares how much money you have! Own your situation and do not be ashamed of your financial status. I often had people in my life telling me that being rich is better than being poor. But some of the wealthiest people I know are struggling with their happiness and some of the poorest people I know are the most interesting, insightful, and happiest people I know.

So, we can either live the million-dollar lifestyle, where maintaining your stuff/image will make you miserable, or you can live a more modest lifestyle along with your riches and be happy. When it comes to monetary items, more is not better. I do not know about you, but when I look in my closet and see two hundred different items, it makes me feel overwhelmed. I would much rather look in my closet and see fifty different items that I love and easily pair together.

Our pleasures derived from material items are temporary. And yes, it is nice to have nice things, but do we really need a million of them. Instead of buying six tops that will only last you a year, why not buy one or two shirts that will last you ten years? While the government chooses to focus its efforts on limiting emissions, they should really be redirecting their focus toward limiting overconsumption and creating laws around the lifespan of products, preventing us from disposal and economic destruction. Their focus should also aim on limiting how much those companies are allowed to produce in a year. I would rather pay more for one item that will last a lifetime than have many items that will eventually fill our landfills.

I would bet that once the government chooses to focus its energy toward actually protecting the planet and not continually trying to make a buck, we will start seeing a powerful and positive impact on our planet.

I am not suggesting that we all need to become minimalists, but we should start living minimally. Showing gratitude and appreciation for the things you already have, such as clothes, cars, memorabilia, and so forth, will give your items a longer lifespan. Believe it or not, those things also hold energy, and your thoughts can positively or negatively impact their quality. So take care of the things you have and appreciate them. A great way to limit you from repurchasing items is by making a mental note of what you already own. This should prevent you from doubling up on what you already have.

Before you go shopping for groceries or clothing, make sure to take an inventory of what you already have. A lot of the time we forget what we have, which can create a lot of unnecessary waste. Less is more. Stay organized and only keep the things that are useful to you or bring joy to your life. Removing the clutter and saying goodbye to those things that are no longer serving you will help clear your mind and give you a better understanding of what your needs should be. A clutter-free home or office means a clutter-free mind.

You need to own your own experiences, learn and grow from them, and be proud of who you are, because we are all special. Monetary wealth will not define you. You define you. And people will love you because of your flaws and your strengths. Not because of what you own or what type of monetary things you can contribute to their life. There is no doubt there are people like this in the world, but these are not the types of people we want around us. We want people to like us for us and not for what we have.

When we stop caring what others think and stop falling victim to all the cheesy marketing campaigns that make us feel like we need more or are not good enough, we can regain our confidence. When we are confident enough to know that we are perfect and that we have everything we need, we can begin to find peace in "not wanting" and let go of the desires that are not serving us. This will free up space and energy that we can direct toward bettering ourselves and our community. It also allows us to become more creative and expressive, utilizing the things we already have to create something new. Just as our grandparents once did.

Twenty-Five

MINIMIZING OUR IMPACT ON THE ENVIRONMENT

Take care of the earth as though you borrowed it from a friend.

I think collectively we are all coming to understand that the planet will not sustain our destruction for eternity. Although it will likely survive millions and millions, maybe even billions or trillions, of years to come. Nevertheless, I think no matter what your take on climate change is, we can all agree that we can do better. It is incredibly important for us to take care of Mother Earth.

The way that I envision our planet is as though she is mother. She is living, breathing, and alive. She provides us with clean air to breathe, food to eat, water to drink, beautiful landscapes to live in. She takes care of us, and she nurtures us. So, in return, we need to take care of her, just as though we would take care of our own mother if she were sick. We need to do something about protecting our planet.

I personally feel strongly connected to Mother Earth and feel an obligation to protect her. Just like our mother, without her, we would not exist. And like your mother, when she gets old and sick, you must take care of her. For what we are doing now is destroying her.

We are overconsuming food, water, material items, and energy. We dispose of absolutely everything, and we no longer care for the things we have.

Mostly because it is cheaper to replace it than it is to fix it. However, we should consider giving life to secondhand items or choose to spend a bit of money on repairing the ones we have. As I said in the previous chapter, once we appreciate and give love to the things we already have, we can then minimize our waste, especially when it comes to physically larger products such as appliances and automobiles.

There are a few ways that you can immediately lessen your impact on the environment that will not cost you a thing. You might even save a few bucks by becoming more aware of your energy consumptions. Start by keeping the lights off and opening your windows to allow the natural light in. Turn your furnace or AC down during the day while you are away at work. You can also switch to energy-saving light bulbs and try unplugging things you are not using. Not only will this help you reduce your energy consumption but also, with today's outrageous energy bills, it might actually save you a few bucks. Maybe even a few hundreds.

Another easy way to make a difference would be by conserving our resources. Do not let the shower run for ten minutes before you get in. We all do it. Instead, turn it on right before you get in. Also, use energy-efficient appliances, and as some dishwasher manufacturers claim, doing a load of dishes in the dishwasher can actually save gallons of water versus handwashing. So, as I like to say, "Let the dishwasher do the dirty work."

I also cannot say this enough: recycle, recycle, recycle. Recycle your cardboard, your paper, your plastic, your metal. I mean, you can get money for it. Definitely recycle your batteries! Recycle your old phones, your old cameras, all of your old electronics. *People!* Let us recycle, and please do your research. Many cities, like my own, encourage recycling, but if it is not done properly, it will still go to the landfill. So be aware of what items are acceptable where.

Instead of relying on your local grocery store for fresh produce, why not give gardening a try? However, try to avoid chemical fertilizers and pesticides. Not only is this harmful for you; also, the chemicals will eventually seep into the local water table, affecting wildlife and damaging our ecosystems. Instead, try composting. Your organic waste will become natural fertilizer for your new garden. There is also a myth surrounded around how pricey local farmers markets might be. But this is not true. Do you know that I was able to get twelve large cucumbers plus a huge bag of potatoes for only twelve Canadian dollars? Our commercial Canadian grocery stores are far more expensive than that. Supporting your local farmers market can lower your environmental impact by limiting the travel distance from producer to plate. Plus, buying in-season produce always tastes so much better.

If you live in a rural area, it can be challenging to eliminate vehicle commutes; however, you can plan a day to just stay home. Not driving for even one day a week will lower toxic emissions and will make a significant difference in battling the toxic poisons damaging Mother Earth's lungs. And remember that even small gradual changes can make a big impact if they are practiced regularly. With change, small increments are always easier to create a habit energy. And once your environmental movement has become a habit, you can add another greenie to the list, eventually giving you the well-earned title of Captain Planet.

Twenty-six

EXPLORING FAITH

Spiritual pride is the main block to spiritual development.

In the book *Letting Go* by David R. Hawkins, he states that religious pride by self-identification with the righteous and having the only true way is the basis of all religious wars. When we identify with religious pride and choose to reject the spiritual views of anyone else, we are belittling the ideas of someone else. The foundation of personal betterment is the goal of religion. No matter if you are Catholic, Buddhist, or a Jehovah's Witness, it is best to respect and love one another, rather than try to prove that the other is wrong. It is not necessary for all religions to become one. Just like people, it is necessary for religions to be diverse in order to serve all of our diverse personalities. As the Dalai Lama suggests, it is not important to convert others to your religion; what is important is how we can contribute to human society. Our universal religion should be love, and I think no matter what our beliefs may be, I think that most of us can agree that *love* is what draws us into religion. Feeling connected and loved and sharing those attributes with the people around us is what draws us to these organizations. There are many religions that have been christened as evil, but I personally believe that they were all instituted on the basis of love. The Devil is a master of disguise and can take on many forms. He is a master manipulator and can fool even the kindest of hearts. And although

I do not believe there is an actual Devil, I do believe there are a lot of selfish/ill-intended people living on this planet who will ultimately do anything for money and power, in turn destroying the reputation of something that was meant to be good.

If you look at Jesus and the Buddha, they both lived humble, nonmaterialistic lives with a common goal of ending suffering. Ultimately, we all yearn to do the same; we just get lost in the hustle and bustle of life. When we slow down and take a good look at what we truly desire from life, the answer becomes clear. Life is about connection, kindness, and the end of suffering, not money, power, or material things. No one religion is better than the other, and if we are worshiping for the right reasons, we should feel full of love.

Rick Warren said that "worship is a universal urge." We all have this seed within us that needs to be sprouted and fulfilled. There is an innate desire to connect to God and a life outside of this existence, where our souls can reconnect in a peaceful place. I often think of life as a spiritual video game. If we live this life the best, we can by being kind, loving, and supportive. We will power up to the next level. But if we choose to be hateful, we power down to the next level. There is always an opportunity for growth, and there are often things we can learn from different religions that will bring us immense joy. There are different foods, music, nationalities, mannerisms, and demeanors we might never have been exposed to if we chose to be hateful and judgmental.

When there is religious cohesion, we all become better. We have so much to learn from one another, and if we choose to listen, instead of to preach, we end up gaining so much more. We become more accepting and more loving. And it is said that when you have faith, no matter what that faith is, you are likely to live longer, be healthier, and feel happier.

Twenty-seven

Nurturing Inner Peace and Wholeness

Within you, there is a stillness and a sanctuary to which you can retreat at any time and be yourself.

—Hermann Hesse

Finding any evidence of eternity can be rather challenging, but in my opinion, it is the driving force behind our natural ambitions to find answers. If we knew what was to come next, would we be able to fulfill our purpose on earth? We are all here for different reasons, and we are all created differently to fulfill different roles in our lives and in the lives of others. Our diversities allow us the ability to contribute our specific talents to the betterment of society. Just like an architect needs talented designers, contractors, plumbers, cleaners, and landscapers to complete his masterpiece, our spirit needs various experiences brought to us by the diversities of others and nature in order to become more awake.

What might be beneficial to my spiritual growth may not be pertinent to your spiritual development, therefore the universe makes things very apparent when they are supposed to happen and to whom they are supposed to happen to. There is always a very strong feeling in my heart when something needs to change or be accepted. We just need to be present in order to receive the information that is intended for us. The whole purpose of our human experience is to connect to something far beyond our earthly experiences. It is to be one with our highest self and to experience love and only love. I think it would be challenging to willingly become a better person if we thought there was nothing after death. Our spiritual journey is what strengthens our will to achieve enlightenment, and it is that journey that makes us the best version of ourselves. Most people are interested in the survival of the body because they believe they are the body, and therefore they need the body to experience their existence. As it states in the book *Conversations with God*, "There are times when you think you are your body, even times when you think you are your mind, but it is at the time of death we realize we are the soul. The tragedy is not leaving the body. Sometimes the tragedy is staying in the body."

We have this invisible vibration, similar to sonar, that helps us connect to one another. No matter who you are, at some point in your life, you have either been positively or negatively affected by the energy frequency of someone else. For example, when you are dancing and laughing, you are feeding the frequency of joy and sharing that joy with the ones around you. Or, when you watch your child laugh uncontrollably with their bestie, they are feeding the universal frequency with positive vibes—in return, spreading love to everyone around them. We are constantly feeding off one another. The more joy, positivity, and relatedness we can experience together, the more we feed the growth of our souls and the souls of those around us.

There are worldwide mediation groups that strongly believe in the invisible power of collective positive intention that can make a massive impact on the overall well-being of everything in the universe. Being highly sensitive to energy myself, I could not agree more with these do-gooders. There are numerous studies proving that collective transcendental mediations can better our overall quality of life and improve social injustice by decreasing violence, crime, and delinquencies.

So, if there is an invisible energy floating around that has the ability to impact the way we act, why could not our soul (which is invisible) live on past the death of our bodies? In my opinion, it will. We are undoubtedly interconnected through energy and vibration, and after death, what will remain is our unconditional connection and love for one another. Nothing else will matter. Our spirit will live on through our loved ones.

As Eben Alexander states in his book *A Neurosurgeon's Journey through the Afterlife*, "I can only speculate that we must go through a life review after death. We need to feel the emotional impact we had on everything in our life. If we were harsh, judgmental and unforgiving, our life review after death will reflect our mortal actions." He believes that we will feel the impact of our decisions on others far more sharply than those who were affected in the material realm.

And not to cause a fear-based betterment system but to know that our lives are short-lived in these bodies and we only have one chance to be a good human. Thus, when we believe that our souls are promoted to the next phase of existence, we might be motivated to treat others with more patience, love, and understanding. Not only because we might benefit from this behavior but because deep down we know that being kind has the power to heal. When we do good deeds to be kind, we can feel comfort knowing that it came from a place of love. Unconditional love is among one of the highest vibrational frequencies. It automatically lifts our spirit and helps us achieve a different approach to life. Our spirit is unconditional love and compassion, and when we listen to what it has to say, we can trust that the answer in rooted in the best interests of all. Not focusing solely on the self but also considering the feelings of others.

Our goal in life should be to find meaning and fulfillment. We also need to have flexibility within what we choose to identify us. For example, if my identity solely conforms to being a stay-at-home mom, this will be the onset of a full-blown identity crisis when my kids grow up and become independent. Yet if we have flexibility within our identities, we give ourselves permission to grow in multiple directions. Our spirit is our home base and is where love and truth are rooted. Our spirit helps us to grow, flower, and bloom, and it can adapt to all different types of environments. It helps us reach the light and bask in the glory and beauty of everything surrounding us. Our spirit is whatever we need it to be, whenever we need it to be there for us. It will always be our safe place.

In conclusion to this chapter, I think it would be good to settle our thoughts regarding the spirit in this parable that compares our spiritual journey to that of a path versus road.

"A narrow road or path is more intimate, more humble, more in contour with the landscape—the way and means with which God has called us to live. Following a narrow path calls us into the unknown, a sense of expectation and exploration, a need to pay attention and be mindful, a willingness to change direction and adapt.

"A wide road requires none of these things. On a wide road, we can venture forward relatively mindlessly and follow the masses. We travel faster, a mindless wake of pollution following us. On a road, we rarely look back. The isolation of the speed makes it easy for us to lose track of our values—what's truly important, as well as our relationship with God and each other. We find ourselves more disconnected with each other and the land. Such a road can only lead to destruction."

Twenty-Eight

GUIDING LITTLE SOULS

*Follow your heart; take risks, learn, laugh; and embrace
your intuition, and you shall never be lost.*

As most of us know, children are very impressionable. Studies have shown that children emulate what they see. Typically, the most influential people in their lives are their parents. It is also important to remember that our vibrations have the ability to communicate and to note that our children are highly sensitive to our nonverbal cues. Thus, in my opinion, patience is the most important quality to master when parenting.

Babies need their mothers or immediate caregiver to embody a patient, loving, and nurturing aura. As we all know, babies can cry a lot, which can make it exceptionally arduous for us parents to keep a calm, peaceful demeanor. All we want is for our infant to feel comfort, and when their energy spikes, so does ours. Nonetheless, if we choose to lash out in frustration, it only escalates the negative energy by creating frustration for the baby and for ourselves. Remember that our reactions to our emotions are our choice. We can either choose to react calmly or choose to allow our emotions to control us. Consequently, if we allow our emotions to control us, our children will think that our outrageous reactive behavior is acceptable, creating a vicious negative cycle.

Keeping calm and patient is the best thing you can do for your own mental stability, and it is always the best way to settle the infant. If you feel too frustrated to deal with the situation, be sure to put your precious cargo (your baby) somewhere safe, such as their crib. And take ten minutes to calm down. You can do this by listening to a ten-minute "Balance" meditation (which you can find in the app store for free), or by breathing deeply for ten repetitions to help calm your nervous system. Take a quick breath in through your nostrils and long exhale out. Make sure your out breath is far longer than your in breath. Do this until you feel calmer. It typically takes me about eight deep breaths before I start to feel better. I also find doing a quick lesson on the Duolingo app helps distract me from angry feelings. If none of these work, call a friend, your neighbor, or a family member to relieve you while you regain your peace of mind. Never deal with your child in an angry state of mind. It is not healthy for you or for your innocent child. Next time you feel overwhelmed, ask for help. It is the best thing you can do for yourself and your beautiful child.

Also *note* that if your baby cries a lot, this does not always have to do with the energy of the parent; it might be that your child is extremely sensitive to their environment and are feeling a sensory overload. This is totally OK and completely normal, so do not blame yourself. Just do your best to support their emotions, because even at the infancy stage, they are beginning to learn to trust their environment and the people around them.

When we emulate patience with our children, they are inclined to mimic our behavior. Monkey see, monkey do. Train your kids to be happy, optimistic, and open-minded. Encourage them to try new things, and spend plenty of quality time with them. Kids are endlessly inquisitive, and they should embrace their adventurous spirits. They are more inclined to try something new in a playful spirit with mom or dad than be told how to do it. Color with them, listen to them, validate their feelings, let them feel heard, and spend lots of time outdoors with them. They are so receptive to playfulness and should be encouraged to explore their imaginations. I always tell my kids, "Don't grow up; it's a trap." As parents, we need to learn to let go of our "adulting" duties and play more with our children. Dishes, vacuuming, business calls, and whatever else you might think is important while you are with your children can wait. There is a time for play, and there is a time for adulting. Do not miss out on your kids; it will be the biggest regret of your life.

Build up your child's confidence by telling them how great they are, and let them know how much they are loved. This, combined with allowing them to accomplish things on their own, is all they will need to become successful independent adults. If you tell your children that they are brilliant, they will be brilliant. Babies, toddlers, preteen, and teens are exceptionally receptive to positive attribute technique. Meaning, what you tell your children while they are young, they will embody. All children are intelligently blessed beings and are gifted with unique abilities specific to them. They are the purest form of life, and they are no doubt the most precious.

When we encourage our children to pursue their desires and remind them of their strengths, skills, and capabilities, they will have the confidence to utilize failure as a tool to achieve success. If they want to be an astronaut, let them believe that they can achieve it! Despite failure, their perseverance will prevail. By putting in the physical and mental effort and utilizing visualization techniques, they can achieve anything they put their minds to. We need to make sure that our children know that there is something genuinely special about them and that they should focus on their strengths and not their weaknesses. For there are many people who will be strong in the areas where they are weak, and where others will be weak in the areas in which they excel.

Usually, if they are not interested in something, it might be because it does not feel natural to them. It might not be enhancing their natural strengths, and this is totally fine. We cannot be great at everything. As a parent, this can be disappointing if their interests do not reflect ours. However, pressuring them to be excited about something if they have no passion for it will leave both you and the child feeling disappointed. They have their own thoughts and feelings about the world, and they should feel comfortable expressing those feelings. Like us, they are filled with their own dreams and aspirations and should be encouraged to chase after what will ultimately make them feel fulfilled, no matter what that might be. Although certain attributes can be programmed at a young age, personalities are exceptionally diverse. It is almost as if we have a preprogrammed personality at birth, granting us the right to be unique.

However, our child should be required to fulfill their commitments. For instance, if they have shown an interest in soccer and you sign them up for a community team. But after a couple of practices, your son/daughter has come to dislike it. No matter what their feelings might be toward the sport, we as parents should encourage them to fulfill their commitment to finishing out the season. This should instill integrity and help them accomplish their goals. Along with giving them the confidence knowing that they can achieve anything they put their minds to, even if they hate the damn sport, it will give them a sense of accomplishment completing what they started. Most importantly, once they complete their obligation, they should be praised for their hard work and efforts.

Although personality might be preprogrammed, our positive influence will help determine their moral compass in life. We have an immense responsibility to instill proper principles in our children. I do not necessarily believe that there is a right or wrong way to do things, but I do believe that there is either a negative or positive intent. We should influence our children to follow their positive gut intentions. If it feels wrong, it probably is. Prepare them to follow their instincts. Teach them that if someone is giving them an uncomfortable feeling, they should trust their gut feeling and get out of there. It is not rude to stand your ground or to set boundaries. There are plenty of people out there who will try to take advantage of those they assume to be meek. Even if they feel it might come off as rude, teach your kids to trust their instincts when it comes to others. And make sure they know to yell, scream, and cause a scene if someone is intruding on their personal space.

I know this conversation that might not be comfortable, but we need to teach our kids how to defend themselves when it comes to predators. My mom often told me that if someone approaches you in a car, run the opposite direction the car is going. You will be long gone by the time they can turn the car around. Also, never approach a vehicle you do not know. If someone pulls over to ask you a question, it is better to keep your distance from the vehicle.

She also told me to walk with keys between my fingers when I was walking alone at night. And she said to go for the eyes with those keys if someone comes at you. Predators are often very weak, and they prey on people whom they feel they can easily defeat. Teach your kids to walk with confidence, be aware of their surroundings, and make eye contact. Be strong and fierce, and do not be afraid to scream and yell your face off!

In this day and age, we should also teach our children to always let us know where they are. You never know who you are dealing with when it comes to online dating, buy and sells, taxis, and so forth. It is more important now than ever to make sure that your child is aware of online predators. Let them know that the cute girl/boy in the picture can easily be some creepy old predator. Teach them to ask important questions and make sure they do their research prior to meeting anyone they met online. Once they get your approval, they can do this through a phone call or video chat. Online Dating 101: Never send nudes to a stranger, cover your laptop camera, meet in a public place, meet during the day for a quick coffee (maybe even bring a friend), and if they are a no-show, they are likely a fake!

Most of all, it is so, so, so important to have an open line of communication with your child. They should feel comfortable coming to you with anything. It is easy to accomplish this by opening the dialogue in a nonjudgmental manner. For instance, if your child is getting to the age of puberty, make sure they are fully aware of all forms of contraceptives. My fifteen-year-old son and I often have the conversation that it is important to love and respect the person you want to be intimate with. Nowadays, it is so easy to find lust and to be lustful, especially at that age. However, it is better to have integrity and respect for each other and to treat sex and intimacy as sacred. Also, confirm with your child that being curious is normal. Try to remember how you felt about boys or girls at that age and reassure them that having thoughts of intimacy is completely natural. Even if the conversation becomes awkward, they will be more likely to share their feelings with you, if they feel as though they can relate to you. For example, I always assure my son that there is no chance in hell that he could *ever* come close to making as many mistakes in his life as I did in mine. And I often share those experiences with him and how those experiences transformed my life. Mistakes are unavoidable, and some of my biggest mistakes have been my greatest blessings. So be gentle with your kids and try to understand where they are coming from. Being a kid is not easy, and they need us to be empathetic to their feelings.

Twenty-Nine

EMBRACING TRANSCENDENCE

Matter and energy are never destroyed, only transformed.

Without death, life would not be as precious as it is. When we accept our own mortality, we start examining our preconceived notions surrounding an afterlife. This notion that God created us is where many of us seem to struggle the most. Asking ourselves questions such as "If God created us, why would he/she allow so much suffering? Why are animals and children being abused? Why does war exist? And why are there selfishness, greed, starvation, and long-suffering?" These are all examples of what love is *not*. And if God is love, why does he allow us to suffer, and why do we have to die?

My greatest struggle in this life has been understanding why an almighty creator would allow these things to transpire? In struggling with these deep concerns, I have often come to the hurtful conclusion that there must not be a God. But the truth is, my heart, soul, and spirit cannot accept that conclusion.

Coping with the reality that there is nothing after death is exceptionally painful for me. However, when I look at everything around me as impermanent, it fills me with a greater appreciation for everything, although the struggle mainly lies in the area of family. Coming to terms with the fact that I may only have this one human life with my beautiful children and husband is a terrifying concept to grasp, hence why the spiritual journey is so deep. The concept of our personalities connecting only this once is heartbreaking and fills me with deep anxiety. I absolutely long to have them in my world forever and definitely beyond this human experience.

We will never know for sure in our lifetime what comes after death, but we should never let go of our faith in something greater than our physical bodies. It is human nature to believe that our souls live on and that we will indefinitely be connected to our loved ones. Can we ever be certain that this is true? No! But I, for one, cannot move forward knowing that we just live and then we die.

I heard a man on TV say that when Adam and Eve took a bite of that apple, our consequence was that we would all be aware of our own mortality. Being aware of our own mortality keeps us guessing, asking questions, and wanting to know more. I truly believe that God has planted immortality in our hearts, and that this is why it can be so challenging to accept death.

Even as a small child and having very little exposure to any organized religion, I knew there was something bigger than our physical experience. At four years old, I remember lying in bed talking to "energy" and internally feeling the responses. Every night up until I can remember, I quietly spoke to someone regarding all my deepest concerns. Not out loud but through a silent prayer. I remember praying for my family, my friends, and, of course, myself. It was not taught to me; it was ingrained in me. There has always been something in me (which is in all of us) that has always known that I was heard and empathized with. It is an energy far deeper than I can explain, but whoever is answering me always calls me "My dear." It is the sweetest, most comforting feeling knowing that there is an entity watching out for me and helping me along my journey. I feel at peace knowing that my prayers are always answered and heard.

For me, it has always been difficult to accept death. Internally, I feel immortal, and I feel like life and my youth will never end. Of course, I have been saddened by the passing of friends, grandparents, and my beloved pets, but I just know we will be together again.

I have sat with my friend/my neighbor while she awaited the next phase of her existence in a hospital room, someone whom I had known over half my life, and I came to the realize that it is important to bring as much joy to these settings as possible. While she lay in her hospital bed after a severe stroke, I cried and tried my hardest to say goodbye. I reassured her that my husband and I would take care of her roommate of fifty years, along with all of her beloved animals. As somber as the experience was and as appropriate as it was to cry, I decided to play '70s tunes and talk to her about everything. The nurses said, apparently the last thing in the human body to go is our hearing, and who does not like music? Once I sensed that my choice in music might be irritating her, we sat quietly in a guided meditation, then I read *The Seeds for the Soul* to her—a book my Oma gave me, but I never got around to reading. Shortly after, my beloved neighbor passed peacefully with no struggle.

In my experience, our loved ones need to be given permission to go. At that point in their life, they are not worried about themselves; they are worried about us. They need to know that the ones they are leaving behind will be OK. Within their sixth sense, they know that when they pass, they will be more than OK. It is us who will be left with sadness and grief and all the heavy emotions affiliated with their passing. But those who are moving on will be free from their emotional restraints after death.

When my Oma sadly passed on Wednesday, January 4, my heart completely broke. Although she was eighty-six years old, she was an incredibly independent woman, and we often visited over coffee. My two youngest girls would terrorize her house while she and I shared in deep conversations about life. My Oma was the most vibrant lady until the end. She took care of her beautiful four-acre property by maintaining her gorgeous garden and trimming her grass. She painted stunning mountain scenes, kept up with all her friends and family, and was full of life and energy to the very end. My Oma loved sipping on a shot of vodka, dancing on tables and sharing memories of her childhood. COVID-19 did not bring joy to many people, but if it were not for the lockdown, I might have missed out on the strong relationship I gained with my Oma. It brought me immense joy listening to her talk about her life experiences, and I was always captivated by her continuous optimism.

Despite suffering a massive stroke and barely being able to communicate, she still waited patiently for all of her immediate family to fly in to say their goodbyes. She was clear to the very end and did not seem to care much about her own suffering but cared more about the well-being of everyone else, even bringing a tear to the doctor's eye by telling her that she fully trusted whatever decisions needed to be made.

Being a devoted Catholic gave her faith that she would be reunited with her late husband and live peacefully in heaven. That is also what she wanted for the rest of us, and until the very end, she expressed how important it was to her for all of us to be baptized, even telling my oldest son, through gasps of air, "Aubry, please get baptized." She cared so much about her children, her grandchildren, and her great-grandchildren that she did not seem to focus much on herself and took full advantage of her last few moments here on earth. With her strong faith and unconditional love, she knew that we will all one day be reunited.

And although my faith has been found within many different religions, I know in her heart she did not care if we were to be baptized Catholic or not. What she truly wanted was for us to find faith in something larger than ourselves. Something that can help us overcome grief and long-suffering. Something that could motivate us into making the right decisions and focus on being the best version of ourselves. It is not a specified religion that will drive us to be better, but it is our passions that will keep us feeling purposeful and at peace. Taking care of others and being endlessly curious will feed our soul purpose on this planet and maybe help us come to terms with what is ultimately inevitable.

Thirty

CONCLUSION: THE BEGINNING OF A NEW CHAPTER

Who knows what is good or bad.

I feel like I can conclude this book with an old Taoist parable. This is the story of a farmer and his horse, and we can all learn a lot from the farmer.

What is good or bad:

>*This is a story of a farmer and his horse.*

>*One day the farmer's prized horse runs away. And his neighbor comes over and says, to commiserate, "I'm so sorry about your horse."*

>*And the farmer replies, "Who knows what's good or bad!"*

>*The neighbor is confused, because this is clearly terrible. The horse is the most valuable thing he owns.*

But the horse comes back the next day, and he brings with him a herd of wild mares. The neighbor comes back over to celebrate. "Congratulations on your great fortune!"

And the farmer replies, "Who knows what's good or bad!"

The next day the farmer's son tames one of the wild horses, and he is thrown from the horse and breaks his leg. The neighbor comes back over. "I'm so sorry about your son."

The farmer replies, "Who knows what's good or bad!"

Sure enough, the following week, the army passes through their village and forcibly conscripts able-bodied young men to fight in the war, but they do not take the farmer's son, because he cannot walk.

This parable really gets me thinking about the things we judge as negative. The reality is, there is diverse enormity of conflicting solutions for every situation. Who knows what is good or bad!

Good things can lead to bad things and bad things can lead to good things. When we label our experiences as good or bad, we are telling ourselves how we should react to life's circumstances. We do not know what tomorrow will bring, and it is only a big deal if we choose to make it a big deal. The best gift that we can give ourselves is the gift of adaptability.

In my personal option, there are a number of things that can help improve our happiness.

1. Becoming in tune with our biological basis for spirituality: Through mediation, nature, or religion.
2. Practicing gratitude every day: Write down five things that you are grateful for every morning.

3. Pick up a hobby: Painting, pickleball, writing, poetry, hiking, or whatever your heart desires.
4. Set attainable goals: Do you want a family, a bachelor's degree, or a promotion?
5. Be more empathetic with yourself and the ones around you: Try to imagine the situation through their eyes.
6. Plan your day, but be flexible with your plans: Do not be afraid to break up your routine.
7. Be patient: Tell yourself to calm down, do not use bad language, relax your body from head to toe, take several deep breathes, count to ten, or walk away.
8. Make time for yourself before you burn out: Exercise daily, get a massage, or go on a holiday.
9. Tell those whom you love, how much you love them: Send your spouse a loving text with appreciation. Tell your kids how much you love them and how proud of them you are.
10. Become present for the ones around you: Dedicate quality time with friends and family. Schedule Sunday dinners, date night with your kids, book clubs, friends night out. Most importantly, put down your device and genuinely connect with those around you.
11. Spend more time outside than inside: Unroll your windows while you are in the car. Breathe that beautiful air.
12. Forgive others and yourself: Write yourself a letter of forgiveness. Write someone else a letter of forgiveness (you do not have to send it).
13. Have meaningful conversations with strangers: Do not be afraid to say hello and ask questions.
14. Be impeccable with your world. Be reliable.
15. Listen more and talk less.
16. Trust yourself.
17. Cultivate acceptance: Acknowledge your feelings through journaling, or confide in someone you trust.

Life continues to prove that it is challenging, but it is our resilience that makes every moment worth it.

Acknowledgments

I would like to thank all of you who took the time to read this book. I feel strongly connected to each and every one of you through this invisible force that has brought us together. Together we can make big changes in the world, and that begins with loving-kindness. Thanks to all of you for reading my book. You have made my dreams of writing come true.

Also, a big thanks to my husband, who has always been incredibly supportive and encouraging of my dreams to complete this book. Thank-you to my mom Silvia, my dad Douglas, and my stepmom Shelly for being so kind to one another and teaching me how to embrace healthy relationships. Thank-you to my aunt Sonnie for teaching me to put others before myself, and last but not the least, thank-you to my three perfect little angels Aubry, Sydney, and Pricilla who have given me the greatest gift of all: unconditional love.

Nikki Weber

Natalie Jensen:

Doctor of Traditional Chinese Medicine
Registered Acupuncturist
Acu Detox Specialist (NADA Protocol)

Lotus Blossom Wellness
nataliejensen@lotusblossomwellness.ca

Kathleen Maiman:

Registered Psychotherapist (CN)
Certified Imago Relationship Therapist
Certified RLT Therapist

https://www.theloveofattraction.com/kathleen-maiman-relationship-therapist

Author Bio

As a dedicated stay at home mom of three wonderful children, ages 2, 4, and 15. I grew up in the small town of Hanna Alberta eventually moving to the big city with my mom at the age of 12. Throughout my life, I have encountered numerous emotional challenges and I hold a strong belief that these challenges have served as invaluable opportunities for personal growth.

For over a decade, I have delved deep into the realm of self-help and personal development and have a deep seated fascination with the spiritual aspect of life coupled with a profound appreciation for the healing properties of the earth. I hold a firm belief in the universe's inherent generosity and trust that it will provide us with the tools and guidance needed to navigate our personal journeys to success.

www.ingramcontent.com/pod-product-compliance
Lightning Source LLC
LaVergne TN
LVHW041229080426
835508LV00011B/1117

*9 7 8 1 0 6 8 9 9 6 2 0 7 *